Fifth Workshop on Fact Extraction and VERification (FEVER 2022)

Dublin, Ireland
26 May 2022

ISBN: 978-1-7138-6737-1

Printed from e-media with permission by:

Curran Associates, Inc.
57 Morehouse Lane
Red Hook, NY 12571

CURRAN ASSOCIATES INC. proceedings.com

Some format issues inherent in the e-media version may also appear in this print version.

Printed with permission by Curran Associates, Inc. (2023)

For permission requests, please contact the Association for Computational Linguistics at the address below.

Association for Computational Linguistics
209 N. Eighth Street
Stroudsburg, Pennsylvania 18360

Phone: 1-570-476-8006
Fax: 1-570-476-0860

acl@aclweb.org

Additional copies of this publication are available from:

Curran Associates, Inc.
57 Morehouse Lane
Red Hook, NY 12571 USA
Phone: 845-758-0400
Fax: 845-758-2633
Email: curran@proceedings.com
Web: www.proceedings.com

FEVER 2022

The Fifth Fact Extraction and VERification Workshop

Proceedings of the Workshop

May 26, 2022

The FEVER organizers gratefully acknowledge the support from the following sponsors.

Supported by

amazon

Introduction

With billions of individual pages on the web providing information on almost every conceivable topic, we should have the ability to collect facts that answer almost every conceivable question. However, only a small fraction of this information is contained in structured sources such as Wikidata; we are therefore limited by our ability to transform free-form text to structured knowledge. There is, however, another problem that has become the focus of a lot of recent research and media coverage: false information coming from unreliable sources.

To ensure accuracy, any content must be verified. However, the volume of information precludes human moderators from doing so. Hence, it is paramount to research automated means to verify accuracy and consistency of information published online and the downstream systems (such as Question Answering, Search and Digital Personal Assistants) which rely on it.

The fifth edition of the FEVER workshop collocated with ACL 2022 aims to continue promoting ongoing research in above area, following on from the first four collocated with EMNLP 2018, EMNLP 2019, ACL 2020, and EMNLP 2021 and three shared tasks in 2018, 2019, and 2021. This year's workshop consists of 3 oral and 7 poster presentations of accepted papers (66% overall acceptance rate), as well as presentations from 5 invited speakers. The workshop is held in hybrid mode with in-person and virtual poster sessions, live-streamed oral presentations and invited talks.

The organisers would like to thank the authors of all submitted papers, the reviewers, and the invited speakers for their efforts, and we are looking forward to next year's edition.

Best wishes,
The FEVER organisers

Organizing Committee

Workshop Organiser

Rami Aly, University of Cambridge
Christos Christodoulopoulos, Amazon
Oana Cocarascu, King's College London
Zhijiang Guo, University of Cambridge
Arpit Mittal, Meta
Michael Schlichtkrull, University of Cambridge
James Thorne, University of Cambridge
Andreas Vlachos, University of Cambridge

References

Danqi Chen, Adam Fisch, Jason Weston, and Antoine Bordes. 2017. Reading wikipedia to answer open-domain questions. In *ACL*.

Christopher Clark and Matt Gardner. 2018. Simple and effective multi-paragraph reading comprehension. In *Proceedings of the 56th Annual Meeting of the Association for Computational Linguistics (Volume 1: Long Papers)*, pages 845–855, Melbourne, Australia. Association for Computational Linguistics.

James Ferguson, Matt Gardner, Hannaneh Hajishirzi, Tushar Khot, and Pradeep Dasigi. 2020. Iirc: A dataset of incomplete information reading comprehension questions. In *ACL*.

Kelvin Guu, Kenton Lee, Zora Tung, Panupong Pasupat, and Mingwei Chang. 2020. Retrieval augmented language model pre-training. In *Proceedings of the 37th International Conference on Machine Learning*, volume 119 of *Proceedings of Machine Learning Research*, pages 3929–3938. PMLR.

Gautier Izacard and Edouard Grave. 2021. Distilling knowledge from reader to retriever for question answering. In *ICLR*.

Harsh Jhamtani and Peter Clark. 2020. Learning to explain: Datasets and models for identifying valid reasoning chains in multihop question-answering. In *EMNLP*.

Vladimir Karpukhin, Barlas Oğuz, Sewon Min, Ledell Wu, Sergey Edunov, Danqi Chen, and Wen tau Yih. 2020. Dense passage retrieval for open-domain question answering. In *EMNLP*.

Daniel Khashabi, Sewon Min, Tushar Khot, Ashish Sabharwal, Oyvind Tafjord, Peter Clark, and Hannaneh Hajishirzi. 2020. Unifiedqa: Crossing format boundaries with a single qa system. In *EMNLP*.

Omar Khattab and Matei Zaharia. 2020. Colbert: Efficient and effective passage search via contextualized late interaction over bert. In *SIGIR*.

Tushar Khot, Peter Clark, Michael Guerquin, Petre Jansen, and Shish Sabharwal. 2019. Qasc: A dataset for question answering via sentence composition. In *AAAI*.

Kenton Lee, Ming-Wei Chang, and Kristina Toutanova. 2019a. Latent retrieval for weakly supervised open domain question answering. In *Proceedings of the 57th Annual Meeting of the Association for Computational Linguistics*, pages 6086–6096, Florence, Italy. Association for Computational Linguistics.

Kenton Lee, Ming-Wei Chang, and Kristina Toutanova. 2019b. Latent retrieval for weakly supervised open domain question answering. In *ACL*.

Patrick Lewis, Ethan Perez, Aleksandara Piktus, Fabio Petroni, Vladimir Karpukhin, Naman Goyal, Heinrich Kuttler, Mike Lewis, Wen tau Yih, Tim Rocktäschel, Sebastian Riedel, and Douwe Kiela. 2020. Retrieval-augmented generation for knowledge-intensive nlp tasks. *ArXiv*, abs/2005.11401.

Ansong Ni, Matt Gardner, and Pradeep Dasigi. 2020. Mitigating false-negative contexts in multi-document question answering with retrieval marginalization. In *arXiv preprint arXiv:2103.12235*.

Qiu Ran, Yankai Lin, Peng Li, Jie Zhou, and Zhiyuan Liu. 2019. NumNet: Machine reading comprehension with numerical reasoning. In *EMNLP*.

Stephen Robertson and Hugo Zaragoza. 2009. The probabilistic relevance framework: Bm25 and beyond. In *Foundations and Trends in Information Retrieval*.

Sohee Yang and Minjoon Seo. 2021. Is retriever merely an approximator of reader? In *arXiv preprint arXiv:2010.10999*.

Chen Zhao, Chenyan Xiong, Jordan Boyd-Graber, and Hal Daumé III. 2021. Distantly-supervised evidence retrieval enables question answerwing without evidence annotation. In *EMNLP*.

Program Committee

Program Committee

Daniele Bonadiman, Amazon
Dominik Stammbach, ETH Zurich
Esma Balkir, National Research Council Canada
Ivan Habernal, TU Darmstadt
Andreas Hanselowski, TU Darmstadt
Hugo Perrin, Buster.ai
Jodi Schneider, University of Illinois, Urbana Champaign
Kevin Small, Amazon
Laura Mascarell, ETH Zurich
Christopher Malon, NEC Laboratories America
Martin Funkquist, TU Darmstadt
Mitch Paul Mithun, University of Arizona
Menglin Xia, Amazon
Motoki Taniguchi, Fuji Xerox
Ankur Padia, University of Maryland, Baltimore County
Preethi Raghavan, IBM Research
Mohammed Saeed, Eurecom

Invited Speakers

Kiran Garimella, Rutgers University
Alon Halevy, Meta
Kalina Bontcheva, Sheffield University
Alice Oh, KAIST
Tanu Mitra, University of Washinghton

Table of Contents

Program

Thursday, May 26, 2022

09:00 - 09:45 *Keynote Talk: Alon Halevy*

09:45 - 10:30 *Keynote Talk: Alice Oh*

10:30 - 11:00 *Coffee break*

11:00 - 11:45 *Keynote Talk: Carolina Scarton*

11:45 - 12:30 *Contributed Talks*

Neural Machine Translation for Fact-checking Temporal Claims
Marco Mori, Paolo Papotti, Luigi Bellomarini and Oliver Giudice

Automatic Fake News Detection: Are current models "fact-checking" or"gut-checking"?
Ian Kelk, Benjamin Basseri, Wee Yi Lee, Richard Qiu and Chris Tanner

Retrieval Data Augmentation Informed by Downstream Question Answering Performance
James Ferguson, Hannaneh Hajishirzi, Pradeep Dasigi and Tushar Khot

12:30 - 14:00 *Lunch Break*

14:00 - 14:30 *In-person poster session*

XInfoTabS: Evaluating Multilingual Tabular Natural Language Inference
Bhavnick Singh Minhas, Anant Shankhdhar, Vivek Gupta, Divyanshu Aggarwal and Shuo Zhang

PHEMEPlus: Enriching Social Media Rumour Verification with External Evidence
John Dougrez-Lewis, Elena Kochkina, Miguel Arana-Catania, Maria Liakata and Yulan He

A Semantics-Aware Approach to Automated Claim Verification
Blanca Calvo Figueras, Montse Cuadros Oller and Rodrigo Agerri

Non-archival: Graph and Attention Based Fact Verification and Heterogeneous COVID-19 Claims Dataset
Miguel Arana-Catania, Elena Kochkina, Arkaitz Zubiaga, Maria Liakata, Robert Procter and Yulan He

Thursday, May 26, 2022 (continued)

14:30 - 15:00	*Online poster session*
	Heterogeneous-Graph Reasoning and Fine-Grained Aggregation for Fact Checking Hongbin Lin and Xianghua Fu
	Distilling Salient Reviews with Zero Labels Chieh-Yang Huang, Jinfeng Li, Nikita Bhutani, Alexander Whedon, Estevam Hruschka and Yoshi Suhara
	Non-archival: Synthetic Disinformation Attacks on Automated Fact Verification Systems Yibing Du, Antoine Bosselut and Christopher D Manning
15:00 - 15:30	*Coffee break*
15:30 - 16:15	*Keynote Talk: Kiran Garimella*
16:15 - 17:00	*Keynote Talk: Tanu Mitra*

Retrieval Data Augmentation Informed by Downstream Question Answering Performance

James Ferguson[◇] **Pradeep Dasigi**[♣]
Tushar Khot[♣] **Hannaneh Hajishirzi**[◇♣]
[◇]University of Washington
[♣]Allen Institute for AI
{jfferg,hannaneh}@cs.washington.edu
{tushark,pradeepd}@allenai.org

Abstract

Training retrieval models to fetch contexts for Question Answering (QA) over large corpora requires labeling relevant passages in those corpora. Since obtaining exhaustive manual annotations of all relevant passages is not feasible, prior work uses text overlap heuristics to find passages that are likely to contain the answer, but this is not feasible when the task requires deeper reasoning and answers are not extractable spans (e.g.: multi-hop, discrete reasoning). We address this issue by identifying relevant passages based on whether they are useful for a trained QA model to arrive at the correct answers, and develop a search process guided by the QA model's loss. Our experiments show that this approach enables identifying relevant context for unseen data greater than 90% of the time on the IIRC dataset and generalizes better to the end QA task than those trained on just the gold retrieval data on IIRC and QASC datasets.

1 Introduction

Answering questions over a large text corpus typically requires retrieving information relevant to the question from the corpus, which is then used by a Question Answering (QA) model to arrive at the answer. Recent work (Guu et al., 2020; Lewis et al., 2020; Ni et al., 2020) relies on retrieval models that learn dense representations of questions and retrieval candidates (Karpukhin et al., 2020; Khattab and Zaharia, 2020) trained separately or jointly with the QA model. These learned retrieval models are more effective than those that use simple word overlap signals (Robertson and Zaragoza, 2009; Chen et al., 2017), but they require the positive retrieval targets for each question labeled. It is often difficult, if not impossible, to exhaustively label all the facts relevant to answering a question in a large corpus of text. Consequently, even when the datasets provide retrieval labels, it is often the case that there exist alternative paths to the answer that

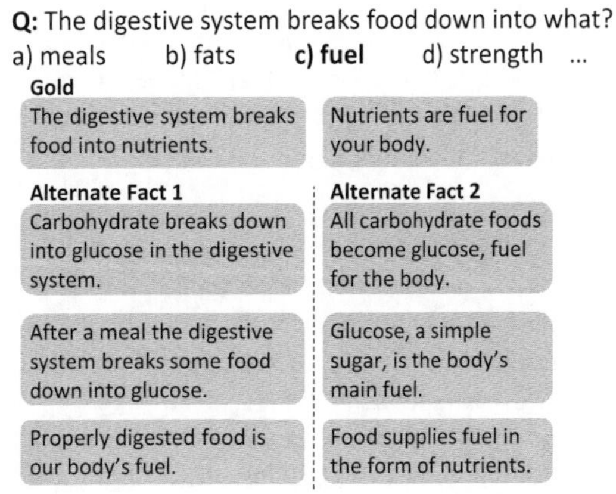

Figure 1: Retrieval annotations (gold) are often incomplete, only providing one of many relevant contexts. Alternative contexts can provide different views of the same information, providing more robust training data.

are not labeled (Jhamtani and Clark, 2020), an example of which is shown in Figure 1. The common heuristic of considering all contexts that contain mentions of the answer span (Clark and Gardner, 2018; Lee et al., 2019a) does not work when the QA task is not extractive (e.g.: when the answers are binary or require some numerical computation).

We propose to address this issue by augmenting the set of labeled retrieval targets with additional candidates that are not labeled as positive, but still provide sufficient information to answer the corresponding questions. Given question-answer pairs, and a QA model trained to maximize the likelihood of the correct answers conditioned on the labeled retrieval targets and the questions, we search for alternative contexts that also make the correct answers likely. Concretely, our search process finds those contexts not labeled as gold, that minimize the loss of the QA model. We consider these contexts as alternative retrieval targets, and train the retrieval model with the combination of these alternative contexts and the gold labeled contexts as

Proceedings of the Fifth Fact Extraction and VERification Workshop (FEVER), pages 1 - 5
May 26, 2022 ©2022 Association for Computational Linguistics

positives. Our method is particularly effective for non-extractive QA tasks since it does not rely on answer-span overlaps.

We evaluate our approach on two multi-hop QA tasks, IIRC (Ferguson et al., 2020) and QASC (Khot et al., 2019), and show that our search for relevant contexts guided by the performance of the QA model correctly identifies a relevant context 91% of the time on IIRC and 84% of the time on QASC (Table 2a). Augmenting the retrieval training data with the results from our search process increases recall on unseen questions, leading to an improvement in the downstream QA performance by 0.5 F_1 points on IIRC and 2.1 accuracy points on QASC (Section 3.2).

2 Method

Overview and Problem Our approach uses the standard two-step pipeline for open-domain QA seen in prior work. We first run a retrieval model that takes as input a question, q, and a large corpus of passages, C, and outputs a small subset of those passages, $c \subset C$, that contains sufficient information to answer the question. This subset is then passed to the second step: the QA model. This model takes as input the same question, q, and subset of passages, c, from the first step, and outputs an answer, a. Depending on the data, this answer can take many forms, such as a span from the context, a number, yes/no, or none of these if the question is unanswerable.

For each question, there may be many valid sets of context passages, where each set[1] contains all the information necessary to answer the question. We refer to individual sets as c_i^*, and the superset of all such sets as $c^* = \{c_1^* \dots c_n^*\}$. As seen in Figure 1, these different context sets may express different reasoning paths reaching the answer, or they may contain different ways of expressing the same reasoning path. However, most datasets just contain annotations of one such set per question, c_i^*. Our goal is to use these annotations to identify alternate, unannotated, relevant context, $\bar{c} \in c^* \setminus \{c_i^*\}$, for each question. These additional contexts is used to augment the retrieval training data.

Approach The goal of the retrieval model is to identify context that maximizes the probability of the correct answer when given to the QA model. When supervised data, c_i^*, is available, this is achieved by training the retrieval model to predict the input that the QA model is trained on i.e., $\theta_r = \arg\max_\theta P(c_i^*|q,\theta)$, and $\theta_q = \arg\max_\theta P(a|q, c_i^*, \theta)$, where the retriever and the QA models are parameterized by θ_r and θ_q. We refer to this initial QA model as the *base* QA model. When supervised data is not available, we can identify the retrieved contexts $\hat{c}$, by searching over the corpus for the contexts that maximize the probability of the correct answer under the base QA model:

$$\hat{c} = \arg\max_{c \subset C} P(a|q, c, \theta_q) \tag{1}$$

Based on this, for each question, we search over the corpus for the top k contexts, $\hat{c}_1 \dots \hat{c}_k$, and add them as additional data augmentation when training a new retrieval model:

$$\hat{\theta_r} = \arg\max_\theta P(c_i^*|q,\theta) + \sum_{j=1}^{k} P(\hat{c}_j|q,\theta) \tag{2}$$

Lastly, we train a final QA model using the gold context, including the results of this new retrieval model to incorporate the updated training and make it more robust to noise:

$$\begin{aligned} c_r &= \arg\max_{c \in C} P(c|q, \hat{\theta_r}) \\ \hat{\theta_q} &= \arg\max_\theta P(a|q, \{c_i^*, c_r\}, \theta) \end{aligned} \tag{3}$$

Labeling sets of facts Because we apply our approach to datasets containing questions that require multiple facts to answer, we need to label *sets* of facts, not individual ones. For this reason, we train our base QA models conditioned on sets of facts, and while both labeling new contexts with the base QA model, and retrieving contexts, we use beam search to output sets of facts. In order to prevent the base QA model from memorizing the gold contexts, we use a 10-fold cross-labeling approach.[2]

3 Experiments

We show the effect of our approach on two multi-hop QA datasets: IIRC (Ferguson et al., 2020) and QASC (Khot et al., 2019).

3.1 Datasets and Setup

IIRC is a multi-hop QA open QA dataset, consisting of a mix of yes/no questions, span selection questions, unanswerable questions, and questions

[1] We apply our approach to datasets containing questions that require multiple facts to answer, so we label *sets* of facts.

[2] We train ten models, each on 90% of the data, and use them to label the remaining 10%.

requiring discrete reasoning such as arithmetic or counting. Each question is associated with a paragraph, and requires both information from that paragraph, as well as information from one or more pages linked to from within that paragraph.

QASC is a multiple-choice, multi-hop QA dataset constructed from a corpus of 17M facts. Each question is written by composing two facts from the corpus, and includes eight answer choices.

eQASC (Jhamtani and Clark, 2020) includes a more exhaustive annotation of relevant contexts for QASC questions and enables a more accurate evaluation of retrieval performance on QASC.

Evaluation We report recall@10 and the final QA performance results that provide a more reliable evaluation of the retrieval performance. For eQASC, we use mean-average precision (MAP) of the positive examples.

Implementation Details Following prior work on IIRC (Ni et al., 2020), we adopt a pipeline approach consisting of three steps: link selection using RoBERTa-base, retrieval, and answer selection using NumNet++ (Ran et al., 2019). For QASC, we initially filter the corpus using the two-step BM25 described in (Khot et al., 2019), selecting the top 1000 pairs of facts per answer choice. Similar to IIRC, we then select the top 10 pairs using a RoBERTa-base bi-encoder. Final QA model separately scores each answer choice using another RoBERTa-base model, and computes a softmax to get the final distribution over the choices.

3.2 Comparisons and Results

We compare our approach of identifying additional relevant context using QA loss with other retrieval baselines and alternate augmentation methods.

BM25: We use the top results from BM25 in lieu of training a supervised model with the annotated data. This is a commonly used heuristic when no retrieval annotations are available.

Sup_A Models are trained using just the annotated training data with no additional data provided.

$\text{Sup}_\text{A+BM25}$ We augment the annotated training data with the top results from querying the corpus using BM25 with the question and answer.

$\text{Sup}_\text{A+R}$ We augment the annotated training data with the top retrieval results conditioned on the question and correct answer. As in the QA-loss labeling approach, we use a 10-fold labeling procedure to prevent memorizing the annotated context.

Approach	QASC		IIRC		eQASC
	R@10	Acc	R@10	F1	MAP
BM25	45.1	71.9	18.0	42.0	36.0
Sup_A	46.1	71.8	39.5	51.1	41.9
$\text{Sup}_\text{A+BM25}$	41.7	69.3	38.0	49.2	40.3
$\text{Sup}_\text{A+R}$	46.2	71.5	39.3	51.0	35.4
$\text{Sup}_\text{A+QA}$	**47.8**	**73.9**	**40.3**	**51.6**	**43.7**
Prior Work	-	71.9	-	50.6	-

Table 1: Comparison of different retrieval models. R@10 and MAP are direct evaluations of retrieval performance, Acc is the performance of the final QA model trained given retrieval results. For IIRC, prior work is the state-of-the-art model (Ni et al., 2020) that uses the same QA model as our work. For QASC, prior work is RoBERTa-base model that uses the same model size as ours and is trained and evaluated on the same data used by (Khashabi et al., 2020).

Main Results Table 1 compares our approach, $\text{Sup}_\text{A+QA}$, with the baselines and prior work.[3] Our approach results in improved performance on both datasets with a larger improvement on QASC over the baseline compared to IIRC. This is likely due to the fact that QASC has a much larger number of alternate contexts per question compared to IIRC (discussed below in oracle analysis). We generally see a correlation between retrieval recall of the gold annotations, performance on eQASC, and downstream accuracy, indicating that providing more accurate context to the downstream model does help with QA performance.

We manually labeled the accuracy of the top result for 100 questions for each approach (results in table 2a). We can see that using the QA model to label data significantly outperforms the other two approaches. In table 2b we also further break down the accuracy based on the different types of questions in IIRC. Our approach works well on *Binary* and *Numeric* questions, where the span heuristic cannot be applied. Our approach also outperforms the it on *Span Selection* questions, where the answer is a span from the context. Although the heuristic can be applied on these questions, it often returns false positives. Our approach struggles with *Span Compare* questions, as discussed in more detail in Error Analysis below.

Oracle Analysis Figure 2c shows an oracle study of the same 100 questions from the previous section to determine how many alternate contexts were available in each dataset. For IIRC, we considered

[3]The state-of-the-art model (Khashabi et al., 2020) for QASC uses roughly 100x more parameters than us (with the results 89.6), but the same model with a comparable size as ours is significantly worse, 50.8. Therefore, we use the best-performing model that has the same size as ours.

Approach	IIRC	QASC
BM25	38	41
Retrieval	39	45
QA Loss	91	84

(a)

Question type	QA	Span
Binary	100	-
Numeric	78	-
Span Selection	97	77
Span Compare	50	-

(b)

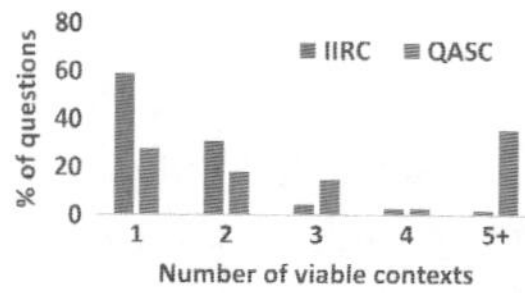

(c)

Table 2: (a) Manual analysis Accuracy of different approaches based on manual analysis on 100 examples for different context labeling approaches, (b) comparing span-selection retrieval baseline with our approach for different question types, and (c) Comparison of the number of relevant contexts in each dataset.

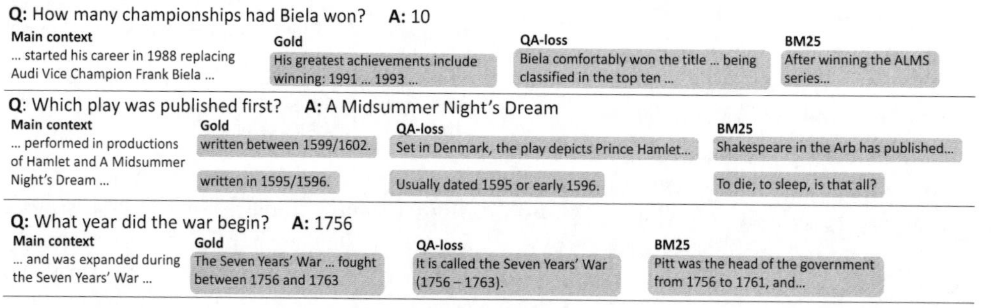

Figure 2: Example errors of our approach in IIRC. Relevant context is highlighted in green, and irrelevant context is in red.

all sentences from the gold articles, and for QASC we considered the top twenty sentences according to BM25. QASC has a much higher ceiling for this form of data augmentation, as can be seen by the fact that 70% of questions have multiple relevant contexts, compared to IIRC where many questions have only a single context. Additionally, many of the questions in IIRC with exactly 2 contexts share a similar structure, seen in the third example in Figure 2. Although our approach is often able to identify this alternate context, using it to augment the data does not add much new information.

Error Analysis Figure 2 shows examples of problems our approach encounters in IIRC. The first question requires the model to count occurrences of an event, but the QA model instead selects context containing a textual expression of the answer. The second question is a *span compare* example. The model has to identify context containing attributes of two entities mentioned in the original paragraph, but takes a shortcut and and only selects context for the correct answer.

4 Related Work

Most similar to our work are recent approaches using weak supervision for learning to retrieve for QA, using only questions and answers. Lee et al. (2019b) pretrain a retrieval model using an inverse cloze task. Zhao et al. (2021) more recently proposed to iteratively improve a retrieval model using hard-EM. Both approaches filter the data using the answer span heuristic. This heuristic breaks down on multi-hop questions, as well as questions that are not answerable by spans, such as true/false or discrete reasoning questions. Izacard and Grave (2021) and Yang and Seo (2021) propose using knowledge distillation to incorporate QA information into a supervised retriever, and while assuming access to retrieval annotations, Ni et al. (2020) jointly learn retrieval and QA by marginalizing over potential contexts. All three of these approaches require encoding all potential contexts together with the question, whereas ours does not have that requirement, making ours more memory-efficient.

5 Conclusion

This work shows that using the loss of a QA model trained on a partial set of labeled contexts to search for alternative contexts for retrieval is an effective method for augmenting the retriever's training data. Our results present a more label-efficient training scheme for building supervised retrievers for QA. They also suggest that creators of datasets for open QA tasks that require supervised retrievers can better allocate their annotation budgets by obtaining retrieval labels for a small set of questions while maximizing the number of question-answer annotations.

Heterogeneous-Graph Reasoning and Fine-Grained Aggregation for Fact Checking

Hongbin Lin
Software Engineering
Shenzhen University
Shenzhen, China
1910273004@email.szu.edu.cn

Xianghua Fu
Faculty of Arts and Sciences
Shenzhen Technology University
Shenzhen, China
fuxianghua@sztu.edu.cn

Abstract

Fact checking is a challenging task that requires corresponding evidences to verify the property of a claim based on reasoning. Previous studies generally i) construct the graph by treating each evidence-claim pair as node which is a simple way that ignores to exploit their implicit interaction, or building a fully-connected graph among claim and evidences where the entailment relationship between claim and evidence would be considered equal to the semantic relationship among evidences; ii) aggregate evidences equally without considering their different stances towards the verification of fact. Towards the above issues, we propose a novel heterogeneous-graph reasoning and fine-grained aggregation model, with two following modules: 1) a heterogeneous graph attention network module to distinguish different types of relationships within the constructed graph; 2) fine-grained aggregation module which learns the implicit stance of evidences towards the prediction result in details. Extensive experiments on the benchmark dataset demonstrate that our proposed model achieves much better performance than state-of-the-art methods.

1 Introduction

Today, social media is considered as the biggest platform to share news and seek information. However, misinformation is spreading at increasing rates and may cause great impact to society. The reach of fake news was best highlighted during the critical months of the 2016 U.S. presidential election generated millions of shares and comments on Facebook (Zafarani et al., 2019). Therefore, automatic detection of fake news on social media has become a significant and beneficial problem. We pay more attention on fact checking task, which utilizes external knowledge to determine the claim veracity when given a claim.

Verifying the truthfulness of a claim with respect to evidence can be regarded as a special case of recognizing textual entailment (RTE) (Dagan et al., 2005) or natural language inference (NLI) (Bowman et al., 2015). Typically, existing approaches contain the representation learning process and evidence aggregation process. Representation process tries to enhance the semantic expression of claim and evidence via sequence structure methods (Hanselowski et al., 2018a; Soleimani et al., 2020) or graph based neural networks (Zhou et al., 2019; Liu et al., 2019) where they utilize simple combination methods such as just dealing with claim-evidence pair as graph nodes. The evidence aggregation process aims to find out the most important evidence which contributes more to claim verification with different methods like mean pooling, attention-based aggregation, etc.

However, existing approaches such as Liu et al. (2019) establish a semantic-based graph, which ignore the difference between relationships among nodes in reasoning graph. For example in Figure 1, given the claim "*Al Jardine is an American rhythm guitarist.*" and the retrieved evidence sentences (i.e., *E1-E5*), making the correct prediction requires model to reason that "*Al Jardine*" is the person mentioned in $E2$ and "*rhythm guitarist*" is occurred in $E1$ based on the entailment interaction of claim with the evidences. Furthermore, we also expect the semantical coherence of multiple evidences from *E1* to *E5* to automatically filter unrelated evidence such as $E3$-$E5$. We believe it's crucial for verification to mine distinct relationships within the reasoning graph.

Besides, in previous methods (Zhou et al., 2019; Liu et al., 2019), stance of evidences towards claim are aggregated equally or some irrelevant evidences are prevented from predicting the veracity of claim roughly via simple attention mechanism. However, each piece of evidence has a different impact on the claim, which needs to be exploited on fine-grained perspective.

To alleviate above issues, we propose a novel **H**eterogeneous-**G**raph **R**easoning and Fine-

Proceedings of the Fifth Fact Extraction and VERification Workshop (FEVER), pages 6 - 15
May 26, 2022 ©2022 Association for Computational Linguistics

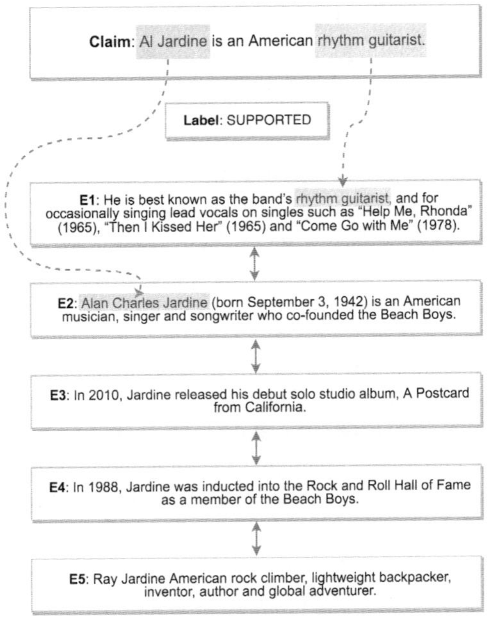

Figure 1: A motivating example for fact checking and the FEVER task. The purple solid line denotes the semantical coherence between each piece of evidence. The purple dotted line denotes entailment consistence between claim and evidences. Verifying the fact requires exploiting these two different implicit relationships during reasoning process.

Grained **A**ggregation Model (HGRGA), which not only enhances the representation learning for claim and evidences by capturing different types of relationships within the constucted graph but also aggregating stances of evidences towards claim concretely. More specifically, we construct a heterogeneous evidence-evidence-claim graph based on graph attention network to enhance the representation of claim and evidences. Besides, we utilize an capsule network to further aggregate evidences with different implicit stances towards the claim, and learn the weights via dynamic routing which indicate how each of evidence attributes the veracity of claim.

We conduct experiments on the real-world benchmark dataset. Extensive experimental results demonstrate the effectiveness of our model. HGRGA boosts the performance for fact checking and the main contributions of this work are summarized as follows:

- To our best knowledge, this is the first study of representing reasoning structure as a heterogeneous graph. The graph attention based heterogeneous interaction achieves significant improvements over state-of-the-art methods.
- We incorporate the capsule network structure into our proposed model to learn implicit stances of evidences towards the claim on fine-grained perspective.
- Experimental results show that our model achieves superior performance on the large-scale benchmark dataset for fact verification.

2 Background and related work

2.1 Problem fomulation

The input of our task is a claim and a collection of Wikipedia articles D. The goal is to extract a set of evidence sentences from D and assign a veracity relation label $y \in \mathcal{Y} = \{\mathrm{S}, \mathrm{R}, \mathrm{N}\}$ to a claim with respect to the evidence set, where **S** = *SUPPORTED*, **R** = ***REFUTED***, and **N** = *NOTENOUGHINFO(NEI)*.

2.2 Fact checking

The process of evidence-based fact checking involves the following three subtasks: document retrieval, evidence sentence selection and claim verification. In the document retrieval phrase, researchers use a hybrid approach that combines search results from the MediaWiki API[1] and the results on the basic of the term frequency-inverse document frequency (TF-IDF) model (Hanselowski et al., 2018b). In the evidence sentence selection phrase, Nie et al. (2019); Hanselowski et al. (2018b) use the enhanced sequential inference model (ESIM) to encode and align a claim-evidence pair. Chen et al. (2016) train a ranking model to rank evidence sentences via different kinds of loss, such as pointwise and pairwise loss. Many fact checking approaches aims to improve the performance of claim verification phrase. Previous work modified existing RTE/NLI models to deal with multiple sentences (Thorne et al., 2018a; Nie et al., 2019; Hanselowski et al., 2018b), concatenated all sentence (Stammbach and Neumann, 2019).

Recently, there are some approaches related to graph-based neural networks (Kipf and Welling, 2016). For example, Zhou et al. (2019) build a fully-connected evidence graph where each node indicates a piece of evidence while Liu et al. (2019) conduct fine-grained evidence propagation in the

[1] `https://www.mediawiki.org/wiki/API`

graph. Zhong et al. (2019) use semantic role labeling (SRL) to build a graph structure, where a node can be a word or a phrase depending on the SRL's outputs.

2.3 Pre-trained language models

Pre-trained language representation models such as GPT (Radford et al., 2018), BERT (Devlin et al., 2018) are proven to be effective on many NLP tasks. These models employ well-designed pre-training tasks to fuse context information and train on rich data. Each BERT layer transforms an input token sequence (one or two sentences) by using self-attention mechanism. Hence, we use BERT as the sentence encoder in our framework to encode better semantic representation.

2.4 Capsule network

A recent method called capsule network explored by Sabour et al. (2017) introduces an iterative routing process to learn a hierarchy of feature detectors which send low-level features to high-level capsules only when there is a strong agreement of their predictions to high-level capsules. Researchers recently apply capsule network into NLP task such as text classification (Zhao et al., 2018), slot filling (Zhang et al., 2018), etc.

3 Proposed method

In this section, we present an overview of the architecture of the proposed framework HGRGA for fact verification. As shown in Figure 2, given a claim and the retrieved evidence, we first utilize a sentence encoder to obtain representations for the claim and the evidences. Then we build a heterogeneous evidence-evidence-claim graph to propagate information among claim and evidence. Finally, we use the capsule network to model the implicit stances of evidences towards claim on fine-grained perspective.

3.1 Sentence Encoder

Given an input sentence, we employ BERT (Devlin et al., 2018) as our sentence encoder by extracting the final hidden state of the [CLS] token as the representation, where [CLS] is the special classification embedding in BERT.

Specifically, given a claim c and N pieces of retrieved evidence $\{e_1, e_2, \ldots, e_N\}$, we feed each sentence into BERT to obtain the claim representation $\mathbf{c}$ and the evidence representation $\mathbf{e_i}$, where $i \in \{1, ..., N\}$. That is,

$$\begin{aligned} \mathbf{c} &= \mathrm{BERT}(c), \\ \mathbf{e_i} &= \mathrm{BERT}(e_i). \end{aligned} \tag{1}$$

We thus denote the utterance as a matrix, i.e., $X = [\mathbf{c}, \mathbf{e_1}, \mathbf{e_2}, ..., \mathbf{e_N}]^{\mathrm{T}}$, where $\mathbf{c}, \mathbf{e_i} \in \mathbb{R}^d$ respectively denotes the d-dimensional embedding of the claim and each relative evidence.

3.2 Graph Reasoning Network

This section describes how to incorporate the heterogeneous graph attention network into our model. Based on the observation as illustrated in Figure 1, we assume that given a claim, the evidence should be semantically coherent with each other while the claim should be entailment consistent with the relevant evidence. Therefore, we decompose the evidence-evidence-claim graph into claim-evidence subgraph and evidence-evidence subgraph.

Claim-Evidence Subgraph Considering that the neighbors of each node in subgraphs have different importance to learn node embedding for fact checking task, we use graph attention network (GAT) (Veličković et al., 2017) to generate the sentence representation of claim and the retrieved evidence.

We use $H^l_{ce} = [h^l_0, h^l_1, h^l_2, ..., h^l_N]^{\mathrm{T}}$ to represent the hidden states of nodes at layer l and initially, $H^0_{ce} = X$. In order to encode structural contexts to improve the sentence-level representation by adaptively learning different contributions of neighbors to each node, we perform self-attention mechanism on the nodes to model the interactions between each node and its neighbors. The attention coefficient can be computed as follows:

$$\begin{aligned} \alpha^l_{i,j} &= Atten(h^l_i, h^l_j) \\ &= \frac{exp(\phi(a^T[W^l h^l_i || W^l h^l_j]))}{\sum_{j \in N_i} exp(\phi(a^T[W^l h^l_i || W^l h^l_j]))}, \end{aligned} \tag{2}$$

where $\alpha^l_{i,j}$ indicates the importance of node i to j at layer l, a is a weight vector, W^l is a layer-specific trainable transformation matrix, $||$ means "concatenate" operation, N_i contains node i's one-hop neighbors and node i itself, ϕ denotes the activation function, such as LeakyReLU (Girshick et al., 2014). Here, we use the adjacency matrix A^{ce} to denotes the relationship between each node, which is defined as:

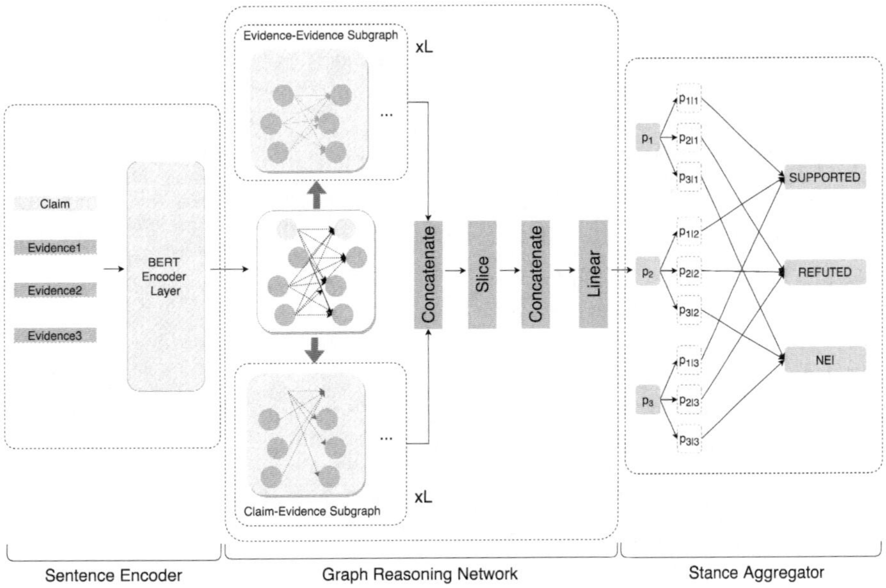

Figure 2: The pipeline of our method. The HGRGA framework is illustrated in the proposed method section.

$$A_{i,j}^{ce} = \begin{cases} 1 & i/j \in \{claim\}, \\ & j/i \in \{claim, e_1, ..., e_N\} \\ 0 & otherwise \end{cases}, \quad (3)$$

then the layer-wise propagation rule is defined as:

$$h_i^{l+1} = ReLU(\sum_{j \in N_i} \alpha_{i,j}^l W^l h_j^l). \quad (4)$$

After that, multi-head attention (Vaswani et al., 2017) is utilized to stabilize the learning process of self-attention and extend attention mechanism. Thus Eq. 4 would be extended to the multi-head attention process of concatenating M attention heads:

$$h_i^{l+1} = \mathop{\Vert}_{m=1}^{M} ReLU(\sum_{j \in N_i} \alpha_{i,j}^{l,m} W_m^l h_j^l), \quad (5)$$

where $||$ represents concatenation, $\alpha_{i,j}^{l,m}$ is a normalized attention coefficient computed by the m-th head at the l-th layer, and W_m^l is the corresponding input linear transformation's weight matrix. By stacking L layers of GAT, the output embedding in the final layer is calculated using averaging, instead of the concatenation operation:

$$h_i^L = ReLU(\frac{1}{M} \sum_{m=1}^{M} \sum_{j \in N_i} \alpha_{i,j}^{L-1,m} W_m^{L-1} h_j^{L-1}). \quad (6)$$

Through aforementioned operations, we get the final layer of claim-evidence subgraph result $H_{ce}^L = [h_0^L, h_1^L, h_2^L, ..., h_N^L]^{\mathrm{T}}$.

Evidence-Evidence Subgraph Similarly to the claim-evidence subgraph in Section 3.2, we enhance the semantical coherence of each evidence via GAT method. More concretely, we use $H_{ee}^l = [\tilde{h}_0^l, \tilde{h}_1^l, \tilde{h}_2^l, ..., \tilde{h}_N^l]^{\mathrm{T}}$ to represent the hidden states of nodes at layer l and initially, $H_{ee}^0 = X$. Besides, the relationship between nodes within subgraph is different and we utilize the adjacency matrix A^{ee} to denotes the relationship between each node, which is defined as:

$$A_{i,j}^{ee} = \begin{cases} 1 & i \in \{e_1, ..., e_N\}, \\ & j \in \{e_1, ..., e_N\} \\ 0 & otherwise \end{cases}. \quad (7)$$

Finally, the output of evidence-evidence subgraph can be updated via $H_{ee}^L = [\tilde{h}_0^L, \tilde{h}_1^L, \tilde{h}_2^L, ..., \tilde{h}_N^L]^{\mathrm{T}}$.

Fusion of Subgraphs To fuse the information contained in two subgraphs, we concatenate H_{ce}^L and H_{ee}^L to form implicit representation of claim and evidences, denoted as H^L . Then, we propose a slice operation to extract claim and evidence feature separately from H^L, denoted as $s_c \in \mathbb{R}^{2d \times 1}$ and $s_e \in \mathbb{R}^{2d \times N}$. Consequently, we tile s_c N times and concatenate them with s_e to construct a new feature matrix as

$$\begin{aligned} \mathbf{s} &= concat(s_c, s_e), \\ \mathbf{p} &= tanh(W_s \mathbf{s} + b_s), \end{aligned} \quad (8)$$

where $W_s \in \mathbb{R}^{d \times 4d}$ and $b_s \in \mathbb{R}^{d \times 1}$ are the weight and bias matrix for dimensionality reduction operation. $\mathbf{p} \in \mathbb{R}^{d \times N}$ denotes the implicit stance of evidences towards final class prediction. The reason we use the concatenation operation is that we think the evidence nodes in the following aggregation process need the information from the claim to guide the routing agreement process among them.

3.3 Stance Aggregator

To model the fine-grained stances of evidences towards class prediction, we incorporate the capsule network (Sabour et al., 2017) into our model. We regard $\mathbf{p}$ as the primary capsule $p_i|_{i=1}^{N} \in \mathbb{R}^d$, Let $v_k|_{k=1}^{K} \in \mathbb{R}^{d_c}$ denote the high-level class capsules, where K denotes the number of classes and d_c means the dimension of class capsules' representation. The capsule model learns a hierarchy of feature detectors via a routing-by-agreement mechanism, which define the different contributions of stances of evidences towards prediction result.

Dynamic Routing-by-agreement We denote $p_{k|i}$ as the resulting prediction vector of the i-th stance capsule when being recognized as the k-th class:

$$p_{k|i} = \sigma(W_k p_i^T + b_k), \tag{9}$$

where $k \in \{1, 2, ..., K\}$ denotes the class type and $i \in \{1, 2, ..., N\}$. σ is the activation function such as $tanh$. $W_k \in \mathbb{R}^{d_c \times d}$ and $b_k \in \mathbb{R}^{d_c \times 1}$ are the weight and bias matrix for the k-th capsule.

The dynamic routing-by-agreement learns an agreement value $c_{k,i}$ that determines how likely the i-th stance capsule agrees to be routed to the k-th class capsule. $c_{k,i}$ is calculated by the dynamic routing-by-agreement algorithm (Sabour et al., 2017), which is briefly recalled in Algorithm 1.

The algorithm determines the agreement value $c_{k,i}$ between stance capsules and class capsules while learning the class representations v_k in an unsupervised, iterative fashion. c_i is a vector that consists of all $c_{k,i}$ where $k \in K$. $b_{k,i}$ is the logit (initialized as zero) representing the log prior probability that the i-th stance capsule agrees to be routed to the k-th class capsule. During each iteration (Line 4), each class representation v_k is calculated by aggregating all the prediction vectors, weighted by the agreement values $c_{k,i}$ obtained from $b_{k,i}$ (Line 6-7):

$$\begin{aligned} s_k &= \sum_{i}^{N} c_{k,i} p_{k|i}, \\ v_k &= g(s_k), \end{aligned} \tag{10}$$

Algorithm 1 Dynamic routing-by-aggrement

1: **procedure** DYNAMIC ROUTING($p_{k|i}$, $iter$)
2: for each stance capsule i and class capsule k: $b_{k,i} \leftarrow 0$.
3:
4: **for** $iter$ iterations **do**
5: for all stance capsule i: $c_i \leftarrow softmax(b_i)$
6: for all class capsule k: $s_k \leftarrow \sum_r c_{k,i} p_{k|i}$
7: for all class capsule k: $v_k = squash(s_k)$
8: for all stance capsule i and class capsule k: $b_{k,i} \leftarrow b_{k,i} + p_{k|i} \cdot v_k$
9: **end for**
10: Return v_k
11: **end procedure**

In the above algorithm, g is a non-linear squashing function which limits the length of v_k to [0, 1]. Once we updated the class representation v_k during iteration, the logit $b_{k,i}$ becomes larger when the dot product $p_{k|i} \cdot v_k$ is large, which means representation of stance capsule $p_{k|i}$ is more similar to class representation v_k. In our scenario, that is, stance of evidences contributes more to a certain category. Meanwhile, we can observe the fine-grained distributions towards prediction result of different stances.

Max-margin Loss for Class Detection Based on the capsule theory (Sabour et al., 2017), the orientation of the activation vector v_k represents class properties while its length indicates the activation probability. The loss function considers a max-margin loss on each labeled utterance:

$$\begin{aligned} \mathcal{L} = \sum_{k=1}^{K} \{ & [\![y = v_k]\!] \cdot max(0, m^+ - ||v_k||)^2 \\ & + \lambda [\![y \neq v_k]\!] \cdot max(0, ||v_k|| - m^-)^2 \}, \end{aligned} \tag{11}$$

where $||v_k||$ is the norm of v_k and $[\![]\!]$ is an indicator function, y is the ground truth label. λ is the weighting coefficient, and m^+ and m^- are margins.

The prediction of the utterance can be easily determined by choosing the activation vector with the largest norm $\hat{y} = \underset{k \in \{1,2,...,K\}}{\arg\max} ||v_k||$.

4 Experimental Setting

4.1 Dataset and Evaluation Metrics

We conduct experiments on the dataset FEVER (Thorne et al., 2018a). The dataset consists of 185,455 annotated claims with a set of 5,416,537 Wikipedia documents from the June 2017 Wikipedia dump. We follow the dataset partition from the FEVER Shared Task (Thorne

Split	SUPPORTED	REFUTED	NEI
Train	80,035	29,775	35,639
Dev	6,666	6,666	6,666
Test	6,666	6,666	6,666

Table 1: Statistics of FEVER dataset.

et al., 2018b). Table 1 shows the statistics of the dataset.

We evaluated performance by using the label accuracy (LA) and FEVER score (F-score). LA measures the 3-way classification accuracy of class prediction without considering the retrieved evidence. The F-score reflects the performance of both evidence sentence selection and veracity relation prediction, where a complete set of true evidence sentences is present in the selected sentences, and the claim is correctly labeled.

4.2 Baseline

The baselines include sota models on FEVER1.0 task, BERT based models and graph-based models.

Three top models (Athene (Hanselowski et al., 2018b), UNC NLP (Nie et al., 2019), UCL MRG (Yoneda et al., 2018)) in FEVER1.0 shared task are compared in our experiment.

As BERT (Devlin et al., 2018) has achieved promising performance on several NLP tasks, we use BERT-pair, BERT-concat from previous work (Zhou et al., 2019) as our baselines.

Other baselines are following like GEAR (Zhou et al., 2019), KGAT (Liu et al., 2019) and DREAM (Zhong et al., 2019).

4.3 Implementation Details

We employ a three-step pipeline with components for document retrieval, sentence selection and claim verification to solve the task. More details can be found in Appendix A.

We utilize $\text{BERT}_{\text{BASE}}$ (Devlin et al., 2018) in our proposed model. Besides, some experiments of hyper-parameters such as the size of pre-trained model, the number of graph attention layer, can be found in Appendix B.

5 Experimental Results

In this section, we first present the overall performance of our model HGRGA compared with other approaches. Then we conduct an ablation study to explore the effectiveness of the heterogeneous graph structure and the fine-grained capsule network. Finally, we present a case study to demonstrate the effectiveness of our framework.

Models	FEVER			
	Dev		Test	
	LA	F-score	LA	F-score
UKP Athene	68.49	64.74	65.46	61.58
UCL MRG	69.66	65.41	67.62	62.52
UNC NLP	69.72	66.49	68.21	64.21
BERT(base)	73.51	71.38	70.67	68.50
BERT(large)	74.59	72.42	71.86	69.66
BERT-Pair	73.30	68.90	69.75	65.18
BERT-Concat	73.67	68.89	71.01	65.64
GEAR	74.84	70.69	71.60	67.10
KGAT(BERT base)	78.02	75.88	72.81	69.40
KGAT(BERT large)	77.91	75.86	73.61	70.24
DREAM	79.23	-	**76.85**	70.60
Our Model	**80.67**	**77.54**	74.26	**70.72**

Table 2: Overall performance on the FEVER dataset (%).

5.1 Overall Performance

Table 2 shows the performance of our proposed method versus all the compared methods on FEVER dataset, where the best result of each column is bolded to indicate the significant improvement over all baselines.

As shown in Table 2, in terms of LA, our model significantly outperforms BERT-based models with 80.67% and 74.26% on both development and test sets respectively. It is worth noting that, our approach, which exploits distinct types of relationships between nodes within reasoning graph, outperforms GEAR and KGAT, both of which regard claim-evidence pair as node and ignore different implicit interactions among them. However, in terms of LA, DREAM outperforms our approach with 76.85% on the test set. One possible reason is that DREAM incorporates graph-level semantic structure of evidence obtained by Semantic Role Labeling (SRL) which may contain more external information. Despite this, in terms of FEVER score, which is a kind of more comprehensive metrics, our method outperforms it.

5.2 Ablation Study

Effect of Heterogeneous Graph We observe how the model performs when some critical components are removed. The specific results are shown in Table 3, where H_{ce} represents the node' representation updated via claim-evidence subgraph

Models		LA	F-score
Our Model		80.67	77.54
-w/o H_{ce}		75.64	70.32
-w/o H_{ee}		77.68	73.52
$Homo$		78.89	75.93
Aggregation	max	77.33	75.23
	mean	77.54	74.97
	attention	77.92	75.10

Table 3: Ablation analysis in the development set of FEVER.

and H_{ee} denotes the node' representation learned via evidence-evidence subgraph. Besides, $Homo$ denotes the reasoning graph is regarded as the homogenous graph which ignores different types of relationships between claim and evidence, evidence and evidence. As expected, with the removal of important components, the performance of model gradually decrease, especially when the reasoning graph is trained as the homogeneous structure, the LA score drops by nearly 2%, which also shows the strong effectiveness of heterogeneous graph. We will attempts to explore the effective result of heterogeneous structure in Section 5.2. Besides, it's worth noting that, when H_{ce} is removed, model still has a proper result, where it's investigated in previous study (Hansen et al., 2021) and an important problem is highlighted that whether models for automatic fact verification have the ability of reasoning.

Effect of Capsule Layer We explore the effectiveness of the capsule network aggregation by comparing it with other different aggregation methods, such as mean-aggregator, max-aggregator and attention-aggregator. The mean aggregator performs the element-wise Mean operation among stances' representation while the max aggregator performs the element-wise Max operation. The attention aggregator is followed from Zhou et al. (2019), where the dot-product attention operation is used among evidence representation. As shown in Table 3, we can find that our approach using capsule network performs better than other aggregation methods.

Furthermore, when capsule network is trained, we can easily observe the distribution of stance of evidences towards predicted class during iterations. We will show an example in Section 5.2.

Claim: One *host* of *Weekly Idol* is ***a comedian***.
Evidence: **E1:** ***The show is hosted by comedian Jeong Hyeong-don*** and rapper Defconn. **E2:** Defconn, ***one host of Weekly Idol, is a rapper*** used to perform several songs on the show. **E3:** ***Weekly Idol is a South Korean variety show***, which airs Wednesdays, 6PM KST, on MBC Every1, MBC's cable and satellite network for comedy and variety shows. **E4:** Many comics achieve a cult following while touring famous comedy hubs such as the Just for Laughs festival in Montreal, the Edinburgh Fringe, and Melbourne Comedy Festival in Australia. **E5:** However, a comic's stand-up success does not guarantee a film's critical or box office success.
Label: SUPPORTED

Table 4: A case of the claim that requires integrating multiple evidence to verify. Facts shared across the claim and the evidences are highlighted with different colors.

Case Study Table 4 shows an example in our experiments which needs multiple pieces of evidence to make the right inference. There are some noisy evidences such as $E4$-$E5$, which are not semantically coherent with $E1$-$E3$, and a confusing evidence $E2$ which may introduce spurious information and mislead the model to predict the label incorrectly. In order to observe the difference between homogenous graph structure and heterogeneous graph structure, we plot the claim-evidence attention map from the model learned under these two settings.

As shown in Figure 3a, when the reasoning graph is constructed as homogenous structure, the model would consider the entailment relationship between claim and evidence equally to another relationship, semantic coherence among each evidence. With high similarity between claim and $E2$ on semantic perspective, the proposed method tends to attend $E2$, which leads to a prediction error. In contrast, when the inference relationship between claim and evidence is explicitly exploited, the ability of reasoning would be further enhanced. Making the correct prediction requires model to reason based on the understanding that "*comedian*" is occurred in $E1$ and "*Weekly Idol*" is a show mentioned in $E3$. Based on the observation as illustrated in Figure 3b, our approach pays more

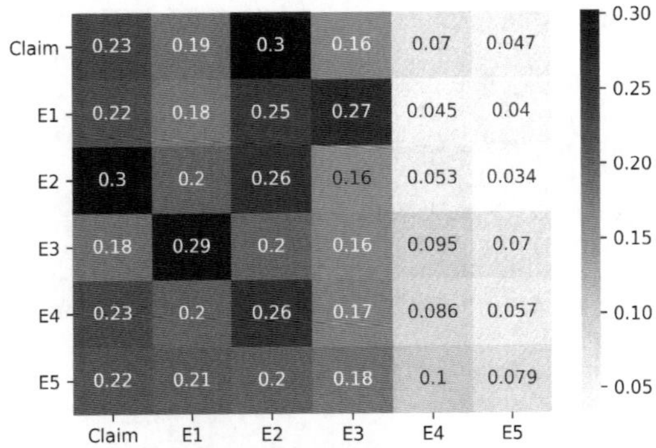

(a) Homogenous graph structure. Predicted label: *REFUTED*.

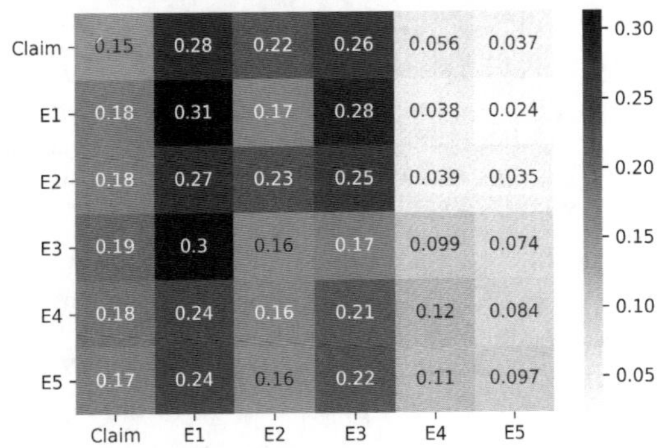

(b) Heterogeneous graph structure. Predicted label: *SUPPORTED*.

Figure 3: Attention map of claim-evidence subgraph with different kinds of graph structure for the case in Table 4.

attention on $E1$ and $E3$, which provide the most useful information in this case, and the label is correctly detected as *SUPPORTED*.

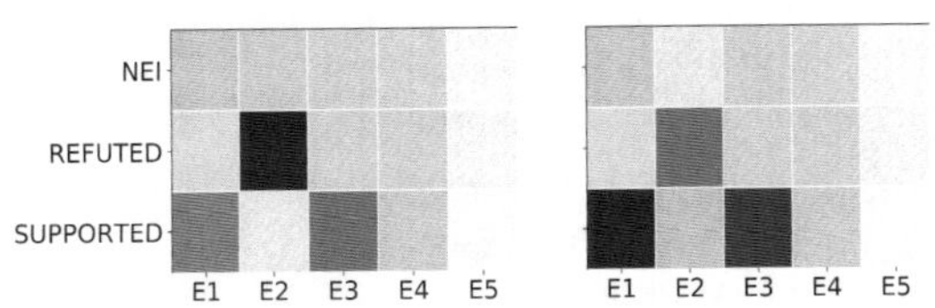

Figure 4: The learned agreement values between class capsules (y-axis) and stance capsules (x-axis) for the case in Table 4. Left: after the first iteration. Right: after the second iteration.

The dynamically learned agreement values within capsule aggregation layer naturally reflect how stance of evidences are collectively aggregated into class capsules for each input utterance. We visualize the agreement values between each stance capsule and each class capsule. The left part of Figure 4 shows that after the first iteration, since the model improperly recognize $E2$ as a whole, the *REFUTED* capsule contribute significantly to the final result. From the right part of Figure 4, we found that with the entailment relationship between claim and evidence being captured in claim-evidence subgraph, evidence $E1$ and $E3$ contribute more to the correct class capsule *SUPPORTED*, which leads to a reasonable result.

6 Error Analysis

We randomly select 200 incorrectly predicted instances and summarize the primary types of errors.

The first type of errors is caused by failing to match the semantic meaning of some phrases on some complex cases. For example, the claim "*Philomena is a film nominated for* ***seven*** *awards.*" is supported by the evidence "*It was also nominated for* ***four*** *BAFTA Awards and* ***three*** *Golden Globe Awards.*" The model needs to understand that four plus three equals seven in this case. Another case is that the claim states "*Winter's Tale is a* ***book***", while the evidence states "*Winter's Tale is a 1983* ***novel*** *by Mark Helprin*". The model fails to understand the relationship between *novel* and *book*. Solving this type of problem requires the incorporation of additional knowledge, such as math logic and common sense.

The second type of errors is due to the failure of retrieving relevant evidences. For example, the claim states "*Lyon is a city in Southwest France.*", and the ground-truth evidence states "*Lyon had a population of 506,615 in 2014 and is France's third-largest city after Paris and Marseille.*", which gives not enough information to help model make a true judgement.

7 Consultion

In this work, we present a novel heterogeneous-graph reasoning and fine-grained aggregation framework on the claim verification subtask of FEVER. We propose heterogeneous graph attention network to better exploit different types of relationships between nodes within reasoning graph. Furthermore, the capsule network is used to observe fine-grained distributions of stances towards claim from multiple pieces of evidence. The framework is proven to be effective and achieve significant and explainable performance. In the future, we would like to explore a fine-grained reasoning mechanism within graph and jointly learn evidence selection and claim verification.

References

Samuel R Bowman, Gabor Angeli, Christopher Potts, and Christopher D Manning. 2015. A large annotated corpus for learning natural language inference. *arXiv preprint arXiv:1508.05326*.

Qian Chen, Xiaodan Zhu, Zhenhua Ling, Si Wei, Hui Jiang, and Diana Inkpen. 2016. Enhanced lstm for natural language inference. *arXiv preprint arXiv:1609.06038*.

Ido Dagan, Oren Glickman, and Bernardo Magnini. 2005. The pascal recognising textual entailment challenge. In *Machine Learning Challenges Workshop*, pages 177–190. Springer.

Jacob Devlin, Ming-Wei Chang, Kenton Lee, and Kristina Toutanova. 2018. Bert: Pre-training of deep bidirectional transformers for language understanding. *arXiv preprint arXiv:1810.04805*.

Ross Girshick, Jeff Donahue, Trevor Darrell, and Jitendra Malik. 2014. Rich feature hierarchies for accurate object detection and semantic segmentation. In *Proceedings of the IEEE conference on computer vision and pattern recognition*, pages 580–587.

Andreas Hanselowski, Avinesh PVS, Benjamin Schiller, Felix Caspelherr, Debanjan Chaudhuri, Christian M Meyer, and Iryna Gurevych. 2018a. A retrospective analysis of the fake news challenge stance detection task. *arXiv preprint arXiv:1806.05180*.

Andreas Hanselowski, Hao Zhang, Zile Li, Daniil Sorokin, Benjamin Schiller, Claudia Schulz, and Iryna Gurevych. 2018b. Ukp-athene: Multi-sentence textual entailment for claim verification. *arXiv preprint arXiv:1809.01479*.

Casper Hansen, Christian Hansen, and Lucas Chaves Lima. 2021. Automatic fake news detection: Are models learning to reason? *arXiv preprint arXiv:2105.07698*.

Diederik P Kingma and Jimmy Ba. 2014. Adam: A method for stochastic optimization. *arXiv preprint arXiv:1412.6980*.

Thomas N Kipf and Max Welling. 2016. Semi-supervised classification with graph convolutional networks. *arXiv preprint arXiv:1609.02907*.

Zhenghao Liu, Chenyan Xiong, Maosong Sun, and Zhiyuan Liu. 2019. Fine-grained fact verification with kernel graph attention network. *arXiv preprint arXiv:1910.09796*.

Yixin Nie, Haonan Chen, and Mohit Bansal. 2019. Combining fact extraction and verification with neural semantic matching networks. In *Proceedings of the AAAI Conference on Artificial Intelligence*, volume 33, pages 6859–6866.

Alec Radford, Karthik Narasimhan, Tim Salimans, and Ilya Sutskever. 2018. Improving language understanding by generative pre-training.

Sara Sabour, Nicholas Frosst, and Geoffrey E Hinton. 2017. Dynamic routing between capsules. *arXiv preprint arXiv:1710.09829*.

Amir Soleimani, Christof Monz, and Marcel Worring. 2020. Bert for evidence retrieval and claim verification. *Advances in Information Retrieval*, 12036:359.

Dominik Stammbach and Guenter Neumann. 2019. Team domlin: Exploiting evidence enhancement for the fever shared task. In *Proceedings of the Second Workshop on Fact Extraction and VERification (FEVER)*, pages 105–109.

James Thorne, Andreas Vlachos, Christos Christodoulopoulos, and Arpit Mittal. 2018a. Fever: a large-scale dataset for fact extraction and verification. *arXiv preprint arXiv:1803.05355*.

James Thorne, Andreas Vlachos, Oana Cocarascu, Christos Christodoulopoulos, and Arpit Mittal. 2018b. The fact extraction and verification (fever) shared task. *arXiv preprint arXiv:1811.10971*.

Ashish Vaswani, Noam Shazeer, Niki Parmar, Jakob Uszkoreit, Llion Jones, Aidan N Gomez, Łukasz Kaiser, and Illia Polosukhin. 2017. Attention is all you need. In *Advances in neural information processing systems*, pages 5998–6008.

Petar Veličković, Guillem Cucurull, Arantxa Casanova, Adriana Romero, Pietro Lio, and Yoshua Bengio. 2017. Graph attention networks. *arXiv preprint arXiv:1710.10903*.

Takuma Yoneda, Jeff Mitchell, Johannes Welbl, Pontus Stenetorp, and Sebastian Riedel. 2018. Ucl machine reading group: Four factor framework for fact finding (hexaf). In *Proceedings of the First Workshop on Fact Extraction and VERification (FEVER)*, pages 97–102.

Reza Zafarani, Xinyi Zhou, Kai Shu, and Huan Liu. 2019. Fake news research: Theories, detection strategies, and open problems. In *Proceedings of the 25th ACM SIGKDD International Conference on Knowledge Discovery & Data Mining*, pages 3207–3208.

Chenwei Zhang, Yaliang Li, Nan Du, Wei Fan, and Philip S Yu. 2018. Joint slot filling and intent detection via capsule neural networks. *arXiv preprint arXiv:1812.09471*.

Chen Zhao, Chenyan Xiong, Corby Rosset, Xia Song, Paul Bennett, and Saurabh Tiwary. 2020. Transformer-xh: Multi-evidence reasoning with extra hop attention.

Wei Zhao, Jianbo Ye, Min Yang, Zeyang Lei, Suofei Zhang, and Zhou Zhao. 2018. Investigating capsule networks with dynamic routing for text classification. *arXiv preprint arXiv:1804.00538*.

Wanjun Zhong, Jingjing Xu, Duyu Tang, Zenan Xu, Nan Duan, Ming Zhou, Jiahai Wang, and Jian Yin. 2019. Reasoning over semantic-level graph for fact checking. *arXiv preprint arXiv:1909.03745*.

Jie Zhou, Xu Han, Cheng Yang, Zhiyuan Liu, Lifeng Wang, Changcheng Li, and Maosong Sun. 2019. Gear: Graph-based evidence aggregating and reasoning for fact verification. *arXiv preprint arXiv:1908.01843*.

A Implementation Details

In the document retrieval and sentence selection stages, we simply follow the method from Hanselowski et al. (2018b) since their method has the highest score on evidence recall in the former FEVER shared task and we focus on the claim verification task. We describe our implementation details in this section.

Document Retrieval and Sentence Selection We adopt the entity linking approach from Hanselowski et al. (2018b), which uses entities as search queries and find relevant Wikipedia pages through the online MediaWiki API[2]. Then related sentences are selected from retrieval document. We follow the previous method from Zhao et al. (2020) and use BERT as sentence retrieval model. We use the [CLS] hidden state to represent claim and evidence sentence pair. Then a rank layer is trained to rank score via pairwise loss. Sentences with top-5 relevance scores are selected to form the final evidence set in our experiments.

Claim Verification In our HGRGA, we set the batch size to 256, the number of evidences N to 5 and the dimension of features d to 768. The number of class capsules K is 3, the dimension of class capsules d_c is 10. We set the number L of the graph attention layer as 2, and the head number M as 4. The model is trained to minimize the capsule loss (Sabour et al., 2017) using the Adam optimizer (Kingma and Ba, 2014) with an initial learning rate of 3e-5. In the loss function, the down-weighting coefficient λ is 0.5, margins m^+ and m^- are set to 0.8 and 0.2. We use an early stopping strategy on the label accuracy of the validation set, with a patience of 10 epochs.

B Additional results on different hyper-parameters

Effect of Pre-trained Models Table 5 shows the results of different pre-trained models on the test set in detail. When the size of pre-trained model becomes larger, the performance of proposed method could be improved. We can also discover from the table that models with RoBERTa-large achieve the best results.

Pre-trained Model	Learning Rate	Time	LA	FEVER
BERT-base	3e-5	35m	74.26	70.72
BERT-large	2e-5	2h20m	75.10	71.86
RoBERTa-base	3e-5	37m	76.54	73.81
RoBERTa-large	2e-5	2h15m	77.38	74.21

Table 5: Additional results of HGRGA on the test set using different pre-trained models (%).

GAT Layers L	Head Number M			
	2	3	4	5
2	72.83	73.94	**74.26**	74.10
3	73.41	74.15	74.11	74.05
4	70.87	72.56	72.87	73.60

Table 6: Label accuracy on the test set with different GAT layers and head numbers (%).

Effect of GAT Layers and Attention Head We conduct additional experiments to check the effect of the number of GAT layers and attention head, which could be important and sensitive to our proposed method. Table 6 shows the result of parameter-tuning experiment and we choose $L = 2$ and $M = 4$ as hyper-parameters settings.

[2]https://www.mediawiki.org/wiki/API

Distilling Salient Reviews with Zero Labels

Chieh-Yang Huang[1]*, Jinfeng Li[2], Nikita Bhutani[2], Alexander Whedon[3]†, Estevam Hruschka[2], Yoshihiko Suhara[2]

Pennsylvania State University[1], Megagon Labs[2], Stitch Fix[3]

chiehyang@psu.edu[1], {jinfeng, nikita, estevam, yoshi}@megagon.ai[2], alexander.whedon@gmail.com[3]

Abstract

Many people read online reviews to learn about real-world entities of their interest. However, majority of reviews only describes general experiences and opinions of the customers, and may not reveal facts that are specific to the entity being reviewed. In this work, we focus on a novel task of mining from a review corpus sentences that are unique for each entity. We refer to this task as **Salient Fact Extraction**. Salient facts are extremely scarce due to their very nature. Consequently, collecting labeled examples for training supervised models is tedious and cost-prohibitive. To alleviate this scarcity problem, we develop an unsupervised method **ZL-Distiller**, which leverages contextual language representations of the reviews and their distributional patterns to identify salient sentences about entities. Our experiments on multiple domains (hotels, products, and restaurants) show that ZL-Distiller achieves state-of-the-art performance and further boosts the performance of other supervised/unsupervised algorithms for the task. Furthermore, we show that salient sentences mined by ZL-Distiller provide unique and detailed information about entities, which benefit downstream NLP applications including question answering and summarization.

1 Introduction

Online reviews have become a rich source of information for people to know more about real-world entities for making purchasing decisions (BrightLocal, 2019). Reviews contain diverse information ranging from general sentiments and customer experiences to features and attributes about an entity. Table 1 shows examples of different types of information found in reviews. Since consuming a large number of reviews can be cumbersome, text mining tools and algorithms are popularly used to uncover and aggregate customer sentiments expressed in opinions and experiences to provide a summary of how the entities are perceived by customers. However, existing mining tools largely ignore information about *unique* features and attributes of the reviewed entity. Such information tends to be sparse compared to expressions about usage, experience and opinions. We observe that in domains such as hotel reviews, sentences with unique features can be as few as 5% of all sentences in the reviews. In a public dataset (Reviews, 2021), for example, "rooftop bar" of Table 1 appears in only 3,026 of 8,211,545 sentences and the attribute is rare that exists in only 197 of 3945 TripAdvisor hotels. Nevertheless, such information is of great interest to users and can be further useful for many downstream applications such as ranking reviews, creating concise entity summaries and answering questions about the entities.

In this work, we focus on mining sentences that describe unique information about entities from its reviews. We call these unique sentences salient facts and denote this task as **Salient Fact Extraction**. Although scarce, salient facts exhibit at least one of the two characteristics: (a) they mention attributes rarely used to describe other entities (example 1 in Table 1), or (b) they convey unique, detailed information (e.g. numeric or categorical) about a common attribute (example 2 in Table 1). Due to the scarcity of salient facts in the reviews, collecting a labeled dataset to train a supervised model is extremely inefficient and cost-prohibitive.

Although there is a rich body of research on extracting tips, informative and helpful sentences from reviews (Li et al., 2020; Novgorodov et al., 2019; Negi and Buitelaar, 2015; Guy et al., 2017a; Wang et al., 2019; Chen et al., 2014; Hua et al., 2019; Zhang et al., 2019; Gao et al., 2018), these approaches have several limitations for extracting

*Work done during internship at Megagon Labs.

†Work done while at Megagon Labs.

The Fifth Workshop on Fact Extraction and VERification (FEVER). Co-located with Association for Computational Linguistics 2022.

Proceedings of the Fifth Fact Extraction and VERification Workshop (FEVER), pages 16 - 28
May 26, 2022 ©2022 Association for Computational Linguistics

	Sentence	Type
1	There is a rooftop bar.	Salient Fact
2	The hotel gives 90% discount for seniors.	Salient Fact
3	The price is cheap.	Sentiment
4	We stayed 3 nights here.	Usage Experience
5	Choose other hotels instead.	Suggestion

Table 1: Different types of information in hotel reviews. A salient fact mentions attributes (marked in blue) distinctive to the hotel or provides uncommon descriptions (marked in red) for common attributes.

salient facts. Firstly, informativeness and saliency are related but have subtle differences. Not all informative sentences describe unique information about an entity. Secondly, due to scarcity of salient facts, collecting labeled training data to train supervised techniques (which is the common technique used for finding informative reviews) can be expensive and time-consuming.

To address the scarcity problem, we propose a novel unsupervised extractor for identifying salient sentences in a zero-label setting where abundant unlabeled reviews are available. A naive approach is to refer to the distributional patterns of salient sentences in a review corpus. We projected all the sentences in a corpus to a t-SNE plot (Hinton and Roweis, 2002) and found that salient sentences tend to appear as border points on the graph. However, we observed that not all border points are salient facts. Many sentences mentioning named entities names or unique personal stories also appear as border points. Such non-informative sentences thus make distributional patterns noisy and the extraction challenging.

Based on these distributional patterns, we propose a novel system, ZL (Zero Label) - Distiller, which uses two Transformer-based models for capturing unique and informative distributional patterns to extract salient facts. It uses a Transformer-based entity prediction model to identify most `unique` sentences for an entity, and another Transformer-based model to filter out non-informative sentences, such that `informative` sentences can be kept. The former one measures how distinctive a review sentence is to the corresponding entity but not to others. The latter one masks entity names in all sentences and drops those sentences that are likely personal stories. To our best knowledge, this is the first work to capture distributional patterns of all sentences for mining useful review sentences.

Contributions. In summary, our contributions are four folds. (1) We formulate a novel task that extracts entity-specific information (denoted as salient facts) from online reviews (2) To deal with scarcity of salient facts, we present an unsupervised method ZL-Distiller, which relies on distributional patterns instead of human annotations. (3) We show that ZL-Distiller leads to new state-of-the-art performance when used independently, or combined with supervised models on 3 domains (Hotel, Product and Restaurant). (4) We demonstrate that ZL-Distiller benefits downstream applications including question answering, and entity summarization by removing non-informative sentences from the pipeline.

2 Related Work

Helpful review definitions. Research community has continuously devoted to understanding which reviews are the most helpful (Li et al., 2020). The gold standard is to collect labels (e.g. helpful or not helpful votes) from various readers passively. Recently, researchers begin to realize that helpful reviews are broad, so they proactively propose sub-concepts, including tip(Hirsch et al., 2021; Guy et al., 2017a; Challenge, 2020), suggestion (Negi and Buitelaar, 2015; Negi et al., 2019; Moghaddam, 2015), and sentiment (Liu, 2012), as complements. To further address this issue, we introduce salient facts as a novel sub-concept, that aims at extracting the most entity-specific information from raw reviews. We demonstrate the real value of salient facts through three natural language processing applications, including saliency estimation, question answering, and entity summarization. Similar to existing sub-concepts, we anticipate the widespread adoption of salient facts in various domains, including but not limited to hotel (Negi and Buitelaar, 2015), product (Novgorodov et al., 2019), restaurant (Challenge, 2020), and travel (Guy et al., 2017a), in the near future.

Label-reliant solutions. Most of existing extraction models (Novgorodov et al., 2019; Negi and Buitelaar, 2015; Guy et al., 2017a; Wang et al., 2019; Chen et al., 2014; Hua et al., 2019; Zhang et al., 2019; Gao et al., 2018; Li et al., 2019; Evensen et al., 2019) are supervised. Although their extraction qualities approximate human performance, the deployment of these models requires a great amount of human labels. Collecting labels for these models can be time-consuming and costly since the process deals with worker education, salary negotiation, and mistake label filtering. Therefore, we propose ZL-Distiller that adopts a label-free design choice while is also compatible to label-reliant solutions.

Label-free solutions. Some label-free solutions attempted to remove the reliance on labels by leveraging data characteristics. For example, Zero-shot learning (Lewis et al., 2020) predicts a sentence as true if its embedding is close to the class name (e.g. salient fact or helpful). Unsupervised entity extraction (Akbik et al., 2018, 2019a,b; Schweter and Akbik, 2020) predicts the sentence as true if its tokens contain named entities, such as person or location. Though these methods have sufficiently leveraged lexical characteristics of a single sentence, they are incapable of leveraging common characteristics of a group of sentences (e.g. salient facts), with which helpful review mining can be substantially boosted. Our label-free solution, i.e. ZL-Distiller, identifies two distributional patterns of salient facts, i.e. `unique` and `informative`, to extract the comments containing salient facts. By utilizing these characteristics, ZL-Distiller shows superior performance in the salient fact extraction task.

3 Method

A summary of ZL-Distiller and its performance comparison with existing systems is depicted in Figure 1. Overall, ZL-Distiller is an unsupervised extractor that leverages distributional patterns (Figure 1A) to identify salient facts. ZL-Distiller introduces two components, `Unique` model and `Informative` model (Figure 1B and upper panel of 1C), to predict the uniqueness of a sentence and to exclude non-informative sentences, respectively. ZL-Distiller achieves better performance when compared with unsupervised baselines (e.g. zero-shot learning) under unsupervised setting (Figure 1B). Though ZL-Distiller shows worse performance compared with supervised baselines (upper panel of Figure 1C), it boosts the performance when used jointly with supervised solutions (e.g. BERT) under supervised setting (lower panel of Figure 1C).

3.1 Salient Fact Extraction

We formulate **Salient Fact Extraction** as a sentence classification task. We choose a sentence to be an instance instead of a review because a review could contain both relevant and irrelevant content. Giving a set of entities $\mathbf{E} = \{e_1, e_2, \cdots, e_i, \cdots, e_n\}$ with n different entities in a specific domain, each entity would have its own set of review sentences $\mathbf{S}_i = \{s_{i,1}, s_{i,2}, \cdots, s_{i,j}, \cdots, s_{i,m}\}$, where $s_{i,j}$ means a review j sentence from e_i. Within $\mathbf{S}_i$, our goal is to find out review sentences that are representative for e_i compared with all other entities. As a sentence classification task, each review sentence $s_{i,j}$ will be given a label of $\{0, 1\}$, where 1 means salient fact. The set of n entities can be defined by their real-world affinity (e.g. hotels on the same street or companies of the same field).

3.2 `Unique` Model

We notice that a salient fact review sentence means that the sentence should be *(i)* representative for the corresponding entity, *(ii)* unique for the corresponding entity, and *(iii)* not applicable for other entities. Figure 2 shows the idea. For Entity 1 in Figure 2, we can separate all the review sentences into two groups, (A) sentences that are representative and unique for Entity 1 and (D) sentences that are also applicable to Entity 2 and 3. Given the idea, our goal is to extract review sentences in (A). And such extraction strategy can be applied to any number of entities. In order to find out salient review sentences, we will need to model the distribution of the review sentences for each entity. By comparing the distribution, we can design a scoring function to rank the level of saliency.

3.2.1 Distribution Modeling

We fine-tune BERT (Devlin et al., 2019) to model the distribution of the review sentences. The model is designed as a multi-class classifier where each class stands for an entity e_i. We first feed the whole review sentence into BERT. On top of the representation of `[CLS]`, we apply a dense layer and a softmax function to get the probability over the entities. The probability $P(e_i|s_{i,j})$ outputted by the model is then the estimated probability of a $sentence s_{i,j}$ belonging to entity e_i. Notice that higher probability also means that the review sentence is more representative for entity e_i.

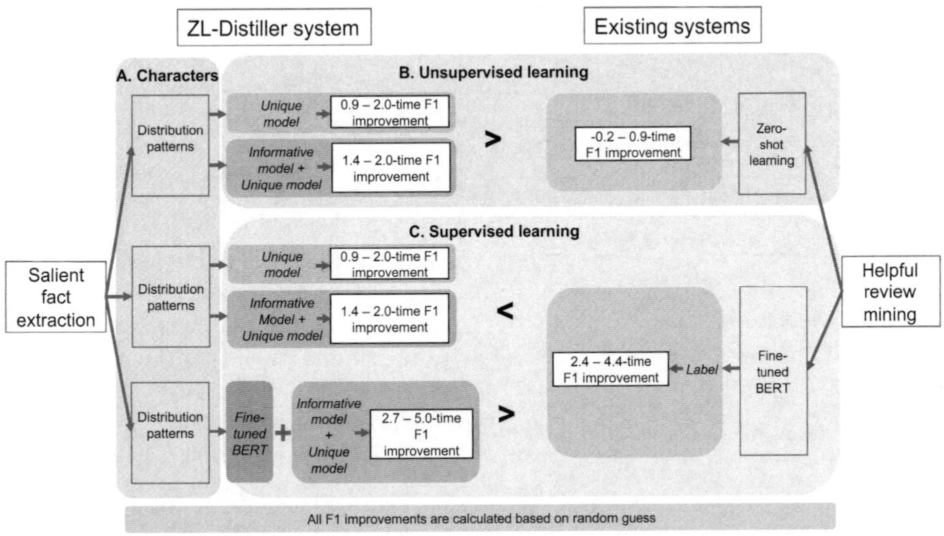

Figure 1: Summary of this paper. Fine-tuned BERT with ZL-Distiller achieves the best F1 improvement. Here when we compare all systems against the same baseline, random guess, that predicts a review as salient at the probability of %positive (the ratio of salient facts shown in Table 3).

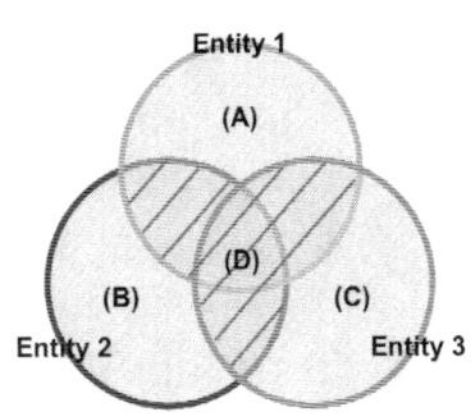

Figure 2: The idea of ZL-Distiller. The reviews of every entity can be separated into two parts, unique and representative sentences that are only applicable for a specific entity and sentences describing facts that share with other entities. ZL-Distiller will extract review sentences that are unique to every entity. For example, review comments given to Entity 1: "(A) The hotel provides free shuttle from/to the airport. (D) I like this hotel". Review comments given to Entity 2: "(B) the hotel is the tallest building with awesome views. (D) I really like this one". Review comments given to Entity 3: "(C) This is the only hotel that offers free parking. (D) A perfect place to live in." For Entity 1, ZL-Distiller will automatically extract the sentence (A) containing salient facts from comments.

3.2.2 Scoring Design

Given the estimation of probability, we design the following scoring function to find out review sentences that are representative for entity e_i but not applicable for other entities $\mathbf{E} - e_i$:

$$Score(s_{i,j}) = P(e_i|s_{i,j}) - \frac{1}{|\mathbf{E} - e_i|} \sum_{e_k \in \mathbf{E} - e_i} P(e_k|s_{i,j}) \quad (1)$$

The higher value of the first term $P(e_i|s_{i,j})$ measure if $s_{i,j}$ is representative for its own entity e_i. The second term $\frac{1}{|\mathbf{E}-e_i|} \sum_{e_k \in \mathbf{E}-e_i} P(e_k|s_{i,j})$ measures whether the $s_{i,j}$ is also applicable to other entities. Overall, the range of the score is between -1 to 1 with 1 stands for the perfect case of salient facts.

3.3 `Informative` Model

We next design `Informative` Model to further improve extraction performance. We explore a set of techniques that can be summarized as two heuristics i.e. irrelevance removal and target name removal. The informative model output is fed as the input of the unique model.

3.3.1 Irrelevance Removal

As shown in Table 2, column "**Review Sentence**", some people would describe their own experience which is not necessarily relevant to the entity when writing reviews. Such irrelevant review sentences could be noises when training the model to estimate the entity distribution. Therefore, we train irrelevance classifiers as a binary classifier using BERT (Devlin et al., 2019) that can be used in different domains. The BERT was trained with 600 manually annotated sentences. These sentences were sampled from the same source as the salient facts datasets (Reference in Section 4.1). The review sentences that convey relevant information are labeled as 0, whereas those conveying irrelevant in-

Review Sentence	Label
Many are still buying the KXTG76xx.	0
I purchased this nice phone for my husband	1
The smaller handsets are the same size as the ATT sets I'm replacing from 8 years ago.	0
They have the same amount of volume too.	0
Could be louder but same volume as my iPhone.	0

Table 2: Example review sentences of relevance and irrelevance. Some people would describe something that is not necessarily relevant to the target entity. These irrelevant review sentences will be labeled as 1. Otherwise, relevant review sentences will be labeled as 0. Sentences are extracted from Amazon office product review dataset.

formation are labeled as 1. Given that we only have a few annotations, we split data into ten folds and train ten models where each model is trained on the selection of nine folds. Notice that even though the goal is to remove the irrelevant review sentences, accidentally removing a relevant review sentence is undesired. Therefore, we take a strict way to aggregate the models' output by averaging all the predicted probabilities. When applying irrelevance removal rule, review sentences that are predicted as *irrelevant* will be removed for both training and testing.

3.3.2 Target Name Removal

When writing reviews, it is highly possible to mention the name of the target entity, such as "*I stayed at the* ***Library Hotel*** *over Christmas and it was a true delight.*" and "*There are so many things about* ***The Library*** *that make it my new favorite hotel in NYC.*" It is obvious that when mentioning the target name of the entity, such review sentences will have high score as they are totally unique to the target entity and not applicable to other entities at all. We thus believe that target name removal is necessary. To do so, we turn the target name into a dummy symbol `[TARGET_NAME]`. However, as we can see in the above mentioned examples, people could refer to the target entity using different aliases such as "Library Hotel" or "The Library". Automatically extracting alias itself is a hard problem in natural language processing field.

To solve this problem, we gather all potential aliases of the targeted entity to augment the list of entity names before training. Notice that in some domains, it is infeasible to gather aliases as the target entity name is too general such as Product domain from Amazon review. During training stage, we feed the augmented list to ZL-Distiller so that it can maximally recognize the entity names. We cannot rule out the possibility that some rare entity aliases will be retained in the comments after target name removal, but most of aliases of the target entity will be removed. In our experiments, target name removal can bring up to 4.3% F1 performance improvement.

Domain	#Sample	#Positive	#Negative	%Positive
Hotel	1008	164	844	16.3%
Product	1015	69	946	6.8%
Restaurant	766	45	721	5.9%

Table 3: Dataset statistics.

4 Experiment

4.1 Datasets

We obtain Hotel, Product, and Restaurant datasets from public reviews of TripAdvisor (Reviews, 2021) [1], Amazon (He and McAuley, 2016), and Yelp [2], respectively. Since a review contains multiple sentences, we split every review into individual sentences using NLTK tokenizer.

We randomly sample 1008, 1015, and 766 sentences for Hotel, Product, and Restaurant, respectively. We invite human editors to label sentences, with label 1 representing the sentence containing a salient fact and label 0 otherwise. The cohen's kappa of two annotators is 0.80. The value indicates a high degree of agreement when compared with the results of existing helpful review annotation (e.g., 0.81 from suggestion annotation (Negi and Buitelaar, 2015) and 0.59 from travel tip annotation (Guy et al., 2017b)). The datasets statistics regarding three domains are shown in Table 3, and the full data annotation process is in Appendix, section Data Annotation.

Evaluation metric. We use F1 score, i.e. the harmonic mean of precision and recall [3], to evaluate the extraction performance. Since salient facts are sparse and dominant label is label 0, we use F1 scores of label 1 for accurate assessment (Li et al., 2020).

[1] https://www.cs.cmu.edu/~jiweil/html/hotel-review.html
[2] https://www.yelp.com/dataset/documentation/main
[3] https://en.wikipedia.org/wiki/F-score

(a) Hotel (b) Product (c) Restaurant

Figure 3: t-SNE plot of BERT [CLS] sentence embeddings (see Section 3.2.1). Semantically similar sentences appear close in the graph. Salient fact sentences tend to appear at borders, indicating they are dissimilar to normal sentences that appear at the center. Some normal sentences would also appear at borders, indicating unique sentences are not necessarily salient facts. The results suggest that we need both `Unique` and `Informative` models for the best extraction quality.

4.2 Distributional Patterns

To obtain distributional patterns of salient facts among all sentences, we use a t-SNE plot to visualize semantic similarity between different sentences. After being projected to the two-dimensional t-SNE plot, more similar sentences will appear closer in the graph. In our t-SNE analysis, we first input every sentence to BERT and use [CLS] vector as its vector representation. We next visualize all the vectors to the t-SNE plot, with salient facts marked in red and normal sentences marked in blue. The t-SNE plots for Hotel, Product, and Restaurant show clear patterns of salient facts distribution as shown in Figure 3.

On all the three t-SNE plots, salient facts tend to appear at borders but not centers. The pattern suggests that salient facts tend to provide unique information that is specific to the corresponding entity. This "unique" pattern motivates the design of `unique` model of ZL-Distiller. Besides, though border points are the most unique sentences, we notice that a large number of them are not salient facts. They appear at border not because they are salient, but because they contain uncommon words such as entity name or personal stories. Such uncommon words do not convey "informative" messages about the entity. Therefore, in addition to the `unique` model, ZL-Distiller adopts an `informative` model to mask entity names and drops personal stories sentences. Further analysis on the differences of salient facts and normal sentences regarding key phrases are in Appendix, section Explanation of Saliency with Key Phrases.

	Hotel	Product	Restaurant
Random guess	0.163	0.068	0.059
TextRank	0.309	0.146	0.100
LexRank	0.304	0.150	0.096
Zero-Shot	0.133	0.129	0.071
PacSum (bert)	0.273	0.127	0.070
PacSum (finetune)	0.240	0.200	0.079
PacSum (tfidf)	0.342	**0.317**	0.077
ZL-Distiller	**0.407**	0.201	**0.144**
ZL-Distiller + PacSum	**0.424**	**0.414**	**0.300**

Table 4: F1 score comparison with the state-of-the-art unsupervised baselines. Best scores are marked in bold. ZL-Distiller outperforms all baselines except PacSum (tfidf) on Product. ZL-Distiller further boosts the performance when combined with PacSum (tfidf). More performance results of ZL-Distiller + PacSum (tfidf) are in the Appendix, Section "Performance of Jointly Unsupervised Prediction".

The effects of `unique` and `informative` models on the extraction performance are in Appendix, section Effect of `Unique` Model and section Effect of `Informative` Model.

4.3 Comparison with Label-free Solutions

Zero-shot learning (HuggingFace, 2020; Lewis et al., 2020) is one of the state-of-the-art solutions that require zero training labels for text extraction. Zero-shot learning can predict the probability of the review belonging to the class, if it is fed with a review and a class name. Therefore, we apply zero-shot learning to the salient fact extraction task. Specifically, we iterate the class name in a set of "salient", "interesting", "informative", "unique",

Model	Top-n 10	30	50	100
		Hotel		
ZL-Distiller	0.222	0.338	0.400	0.415
BERT	**0.356**	0.585	**0.588**	**0.459**
ZL-Distiller +BERT	**0.356**	**0.615**	0.565	**0.459**
		Product		
ZL-Distiller	0.276	0.245	0.348	0.269
BERT	**0.345**	0.367	0.319	0.269
ZL-Distiller +BERT	**0.345**	**0.408**	**0.377**	**0.286**
		Restaurant		
ZL-Distiller	0.200	**0.400**	**0.267**	**0.182**
BERT	0.200	0.200	0.167	0.091
ZL-Distiller +BERT	0.200	0.300	**0.267**	**0.182**

Table 5: Performance of supervised learning (i.e. BERT and ZL-Distiller + BERT) using domain-specific labels. Best F1 scores are marked in bold.

and "concrete", and pick the class name that offers the best extraction performance. When evaluating a class name, we vary the prediction threshold from 1 to 0, and report the highest F1 score. We use HuggingFace implementation (HuggingFace, 2020) of zero-shot learning (Lewis et al., 2020) for experiments.

In addition to zero-shot learning, we also deploy popular text summarization algorithms, which are TextRank (Mihalcea and Tarau, 2004), LexRank (Erkan and Radev, 2004), and three variants of PacSum (bert/finetune/tfidf) (Zheng and Lapata, 2019) for comparison. These algorithms select informative sentences to represent long text so their outputs naturally form a set of candidate salient facts.

We present F1 scores of all methods in Table 4. According to the results, ZL-Distiller shows comparable or better performance compared with existing methods, consistently on Hotel, Product, and Restaurant. Furthermore, we combine the prediction scores of ZL-Distiller and PacSum (tfidf) by taking dot product for every sentence. We observe that such combination leads to the highest F1 scores on all three datasets. The results suggests that ZL-Distiller serves as a new strong baseline for salient fact extraction. Meanwhile, ZL-Distiller can work with existing baselines to achieve the best performance.

4.4 Performance of Jointly Supervised prediction

ZL-Distiller can extract salient facts in unsupervised manner where data labels are absent. Since ZL-Distiller captures distributional patterns, we then investigate whether ZL-Distiller is still useful in supervised manner where data labels are present. Briefly, we use BERT with data labels as the representative supervised solution. Next, we combine BERT prediction scores with ZL-Distiller prediction scores, by taking products of BERT and ZL-Distiller scores and, then, rank sentences by product scores. We denote this combination as ZL-Distiller + BERT. Finally, we take the top-n as the predicted salient facts and then return F1 scores when setting top-n with various number, i.e. 10, 30, 50, and 100.

We present the F1 scores of ZL-Distiller, BERT, and ZL-Distiller + BERT in Table 5. As expected, ZL-Distiller F1 scores are lower than BERT on Hotel and Product as ZL-Distiller does not use domain-specific labels. However, ZL-Distiller shows better performance than BERT on Restaurant. The reason is that Restaurant has extremely low ratio of salient facts (i.e. 5.9%, as shown in Table 3), for which the number of salient facts for training is insufficient. The results suggest that ZL-Distiller is effective when there are no or insufficient data labels.

When there are sufficient labels (e.g. on Hotel and Product), ZL-Distiller performs worse than supervised solution (i.e. BERT). However, ZL-Distiller is still helpful, indicated by the results that ZL-Distiller + BERT achieves better F1 scores than BERT on all three datasets. The highest F1 improvement is 10%, 18%, and 100%, on Hotel, Product, and Restaurant, respectively, as shown in Table 5. Such improvement is general to various domains and this is because that ZL-Distiller can always capture distributional patterns as discussed in Section 4.2.

5 Application

In this section, we demonstrate the effect of salient facts in downstream NLP applications. We apply salient fact extraction in company reviews, and select three downstream applications, including review saliency estimation, question answering, and company summarization. We used ZL-Distiller + BERT (denoted as saliency prediction model) to obtain salient facts as inputs for downstream applications.

5.1 Saliency Estimation

An important application of salient fact extraction is saliency estimation, which returns the probabilities of a text being salient and non-salient. To perform saliency estimation, we deploy our saliency prediction model to evaluate two reviews of Google

Google review	Pos.	Neg.
When a Google employee passes away, surviving spouse receives 50% of their salary for the next 10 years.	0.65	0.39
awesome place to work, great salary, smart people.	0.02	0.99

Table 6: Saliency estimation of a raw review in terms of saliency (i.e. Pos.) and non-saliency (i.e. Neg.) scores.

Question	Salient	Raw
How long is parental leave?	12 weeks	nice amount of leave
How much would company pay for health insurance?	90%	401k

Table 7: Question answering based on Google reviews using DistilBERT (Sanh et al., 2019).

and show the probabilities in Table 6. The first review reveals a rare company policy (i.e. death benefit) and numeric descriptions (i.e. 50% salary and 10 years), which are considered unique information. The model gives a higher probability of salient (i.e. 0.65) than non-salient (i.e. 0.39), suggesting that saliency prediction model can appropriately rank unique sentences. The second review discusses common attributes such as work, salary, and people and uses sentimental descriptions like awesome and great, which are considered as non-unique information. The model predicts a lower probability of salient (i.e. 0.02) than non-saliency (i.e. 0.99), suggesting that saliency prediction model can rank non-unique sentences. Taken together, these saliency estimation probabilities serve as good references for readers to select or rank raw reviews.

5.2 Question Answering

Question answering (QA) tasks (such as SQuAD 1.0 and 2.0), take a knowledge-seeking question and a text context as inputs and then retrieves answer for the question in the context. Though the process is straightforward, application of QA to reviews meets a challenge, which is widespread general comments (e.g. sentiments) that lead to wrong answers. To overcome this challenge, we use saliency prediction model to prioritize informative reviews. In brief, we prepare two contexts using different sentences (i.e. salient facts and raw reviews) and input two questions (i.e. "How long is parental leave" and "How much would company pay for health insurance") for both contexts.

Googlers can relax after a long day by braving the rock climbing wall, playing billiards, or just relaxing in a self-controlled massage chair. Google is paying out my unvested options and RSUs and gave me a grant of GSUs to boot.
Awesome place to work, great salary, smart people, lots of happy hours and the free food is as great as everyone says it is. Too much emphasis on work life balance. Can really make a difference in the world.

Table 8: Summary of Google using salient facts (up) and raw reviews (down). Salient facts enable finer-grained summarization that presents specific attributes (e.g. rock climbing wall) of Google rather than general attributes (e.g. work life balance) of Company class.

We then use HuggingFace question answering engine (Face, 2020; Sanh et al., 2019) to look for answers in contexts to obtain company knowledge. Our results show that salient facts context returns higher-quality answers than raw reviews context. For example, for the question "How long is parental leave", salient facts return an objective and unbiased answer (i.e. 12 weeks), whereas raw reviews return a subjective and biased answer (i.e. nice amount of leave). More comparative results are shown in Table 7. These results suggest that salient facts enable accurate question answering over reviews, where objective and subjective texts are mixed.

5.3 Entity Summarization

According to our results, salient facts represent a collection of unique sentences in the reviews. In addition to their uniqueness, we also find that salient facts can serve as ingredients for high-quality entity summarization. We compare two summaries of Google reviews (shown in Table 8) based on salient facts and raw reviews, respectively. We use BART (Lewis et al., 2020) as summarizer and set the expected number of words to 50. The results show that salient facts based summary is more specific to the entity as it reveals finer-grained attributes (e.g. rock climbing wall). Moreover, salient facts based summary is unbiased as it seldom contains sentimental words (e.g. awesome and great). Contrastively, raw reviews based summary mentions commonsense attributes (e.g. work and salary) and sentimental words (e.g. awesome and great) more frequently. Therefore, these results suggest that salient facts based summary will be more favorable for readers who are looking for informative and unbiased entity summarization.

6 Conclusion

In this paper, we propose to extract salient facts from online reviews. To achieve this goal, we develop ZL-Distiller, which is the first-of-its-kind system for salient fact extraction. ZL-Distiller does not require human labels, but labels can further boosts its performance. To prove that salient facts can be applied to popular real-world applications, we conduct a study on raw company reviews, which demonstrates that salient facts can improve the quality of downstream applications, including saliency estimation, question answering and company summarization. These results implicate the feasibility of salient fact extraction in real-world text corpus including company reviews, which consist of both salient and non-salient contents. Our practice suggests that the general-purpose salient fact extraction has a substantial effect on existing text-based applications for diverse domains.

References

Alan Akbik, Tanja Bergmann, Duncan Blythe, Kashif Rasul, Stefan Schweter, and Roland Vollgraf. 2019a. Flair: An easy-to-use framework for state-of-the-art nlp. In NAACL, pages 54–59.

Alan Akbik, Tanja Bergmann, and Roland Vollgraf. 2019b. Pooled contextualized embeddings for named entity recognition. In NAACL, page 724–728.

Alan Akbik, Duncan Blythe, and Roland Vollgraf. 2018. Contextual string embeddings for sequence labeling. In COLING, pages 1638–1649.

BrightLocal. 2019. https://www.brightlocal.com/research/local-consumer-review-survey/. Local Consumer Review Survey.

Yelp Dataset Challenge. 2020. https://www.yelp.com/dataset/documentation/main. In YELP.

Ning Chen, Jialiu Lin, Steven C. H. Hoi, Xiaokui Xiao, and Boshen Zhang. 2014. Ar-miner: mining informative reviews for developers from mobile app marketplace. In ICSE, pages 767–778.

Jacob Devlin, Ming-Wei Chang, Kenton Lee, and Kristina Toutanova. 2019. BERT: pre-training of deep bidirectional transformers for language understanding. In NAACL-HLT, pages 4171–4186.

Günes Erkan and Dragomir R. Radev. 2004. Lexrank: Graph-based lexical centrality as salience in text summarization. JAIR, 22:457–479.

Sara Evensen, Aaron Feng, Alon Y. Halevy, Jinfeng Li, Vivian Li, Yuliang Li, Huining Liu, George A. Mihaila, John Morales, Natalie Nuno, Ekaterina Pavlovic, Wang-Chiew Tan, and Xiaolan Wang. 2019. Voyageur: An experiential travel search engine. In WWW, pages 3511–5. ACM.

Hugging Face. 2020. https://huggingface.co/distilbert-base-uncased-distilled-squad. Question Answering.

Cuiyun Gao, Jichuan Zeng, Michael R. Lyu, and Irwin King. 2018. Online app review analysis for identifying emerging issues. In ICSE, pages 48–58.

Ido Guy, Avihai Mejer, Alexander Nus, and Fiana Raiber. 2017a. Extracting and ranking travel tips from user-generated reviews. In WWW, pages 987–996.

Ido Guy, Avihai Mejer, Alexander Nus, and Fiana Raiber. 2017b. Extracting and ranking travel tips from user-generated reviews. In WWW, pages 987–996.

Ruining He and Julian McAuley. 2016. Ups and downs: Modeling the visual evolution of fashion trends with one-class collaborative filtering. In WWW, pages 507–517.

Geoffrey E. Hinton and Sam T. Roweis. 2002. Stochastic neighbor embedding. In NIPS, pages 833–840.

Sharon Hirsch, Slava Novgorodov, Ido Guy, and Alexander Nus. 2021. Generating tips from product reviews. In WSDM, pages 310–318. ACM.

Xinyu Hua, Mitko Nikolov, Nikhil Badugu, and Lu Wang. 2019. Argument mining for understanding peer reviews. In NAACL-HLT, pages 2131–2137.

HuggingFace. 2020. https://huggingface.co/zero-shot/. Bart MNLI Zero Shot Topic Classification.

Diederik P Kingma and Jimmy Ba. 2014. Adam: A method for stochastic optimization. arXiv:1412.6980.

Mike Lewis, Yinhan Liu, Naman Goyal, Marjan Ghazvininejad, Abdelrahman Mohamed, Omer Levy, Veselin Stoyanov, and Luke Zettlemoyer. 2020. BART: denoising sequence-to-sequence pre-training for natural language generation, translation, and comprehension. In ACL, pages 7871–7880.

Jinfeng Li, Yuliang Li, Xiaolan Wang, and Wang-Chiew Tan. 2020. Deep or simple models for semantic tagging? it depends on your data. VLDB, 13(11):2549–2562.

Yuliang Li, Aaron Feng, Jinfeng Li, Saran Mumick, Alon Y. Halevy, Vivian Li, and Wang-Chiew Tan. 2019. Subjective databases. volume 12, pages 1330–1343.

Bing Liu. 2012. Sentiment analysis and opinion mining. Synthesis Lectures on Human Language Technologies.

LMScorer. 2018. Language model scorer. https://github.com/simonepri/lm-scorer.

Rada Mihalcea and Paul Tarau. 2004. Textrank: Bringing order into text. In EMNLP, pages 404–411. ACL.

Samaneh Moghaddam. 2015. Beyond sentiment analysis: Mining defects and improvements from customer feedback. In ECIR, pages 400–410.

Sapna Negi and Paul Buitelaar. 2015. Towards the extraction of customer-to-customer suggestions from reviews. In EMNLP, pages 2159–2167.

Sapna Negi, Tobias Daudert, and Paul Buitelaar. 2019. Semeval-2019 task 9: Suggestion mining from online reviews and forums. In SemEval@NAACL-HLT, pages 877–887.

Slava Novgorodov, Guy Elad, Ido Guy, and Kira Radinsky. 2019. Generating product descriptions from user reviews. In WWW, pages 1354–1364.

Alec Radford, Jeff Wu, Rewon Child, David Luan, Dario Amodei, and Ilya Sutskever. 2019. Language models are unsupervised multitask learners. Semantic Scholar.

TripAdvisor Hotel Reviews. 2021. https://www.cs.cmu.edu/~jiweil/html/hotel-review.html. In TripAdvisor.

Victor Sanh, Lysandre Debut, Julien Chaumond, and Thomas Wolf. 2019. Distilbert, a distilled version of BERT: smaller, faster, cheaper and lighter. CoRR, abs/1910.01108.

Stefan Schweter and Alan Akbik. 2020. Flert: Document-level features for named entity recognition.

Shaohua Wang, NhatHai Phan, Yan Wang, and Yong Zhao. 2019. Extracting API tips from developer question and answer websites. In MSR, pages 321–332.

Xuan Zhang, Zhilei Qiao, Aman Ahuja, Weiguo Fan, Edward A. Fox, and Chandan K. Reddy. 2019. Discovering product defects and solutions from online user generated contents. In WWW, pages 3441–3447.

Hao Zheng and Mirella Lapata. 2019. Sentence centrality revisited for unsupervised summarization. In ACL, pages 6236–6247.

Appendix

Non-informative Sentences Filtering

Recently large-scale pre-trained models (e.g. GPT-2 or BERT) have been used to select informative words. During pre-training, these models learned the informativeness of individual words in human vocabulary by reading massive natural texts such as Wikipedia articles. In GPT-2 (Radford et al., 2019), for example, the informative score of individual word in "There is a rooftop bar" is 0.00007, 0.26, 0.23, 0.00001, and 0.00037, respectively[4]. A lower score indicates more informativeness and adjectives (e.g. rooftop) or nouns (e.g. bar) usually show lower scores than stop words (e.g. is). With this favorable feature, pre-trained models can be used to rank sentences by their token informativeness.

Given pre-trained models can perceive the informativeness of individual words in a sentence, they can be used to filter out non-informative sentences. We use GPT-2, a representative pre-trained model, for the filtering. Specifically, for every sentence, we use GPT-2 to obtain informativeness scores of its tokens, then take product of scores. We sort all the sentences by the product scores and select top 20% sentences that have the highest scores. Since higher score means less informativeness, the top 20% sentences represent the most non-informative sentences and will be excluded from datasets.

To evaluate the effect of non-informative sentences filtering, we report the ratio of salient facts before and after filtering. Before filtering, the ratio is 16.3%, 6.8%, and 5.9% in Hotel, Product, and Restaurant dataset, respectively. After filtering, the ratio is 19.1%, 8.1%, and 6.1%, respectively. The ratio of salient facts increases in all of the three datasets. The results indicate that pre-trained models can effectively exclude non-informative sentences from datasets to boost the ratios of salient facts.

Implementation Details

In this section, we describe the training detail of the proposed model.

`Unique` Model. HuggingFace's implementation[5] of BERT is used for our `Unique` model to estimator the probability over review sentences. When fine-tuning the model, we use Adam (Kingma and Ba, 2014) as the optimizer with batch size of 64 and learning rate of 1e-5. The model is trained with the early stop mechanism where the training will end when there is no improvement on accuracy for three epochs. The model with the best accuracy is kept for testing. For each domain, we randomly sample ten entities for training, resulting in a total of training instances used for Hotel, Product, and Restaurant are 95,454, 44,560, and 356,505, respectively.

Irrelevance Classifier. Same as the `Unique` model, the HuggingFace's implementation of BERT is used for irrelevance classifier. As an ensemble model, a total of ten models is trained where each model is trained on nine-fold of data. The Adam (Kingma and Ba, 2014) is used as the optimizer with a batch size of 64 and a learning rate of 1e-6. The model is trained with the early stop mechanism where after 100 epochs, the training will end when there is no improvement on accuracy for five epochs. The model with the best accuracy is then kept. The overall ensemble model will take the average of the probabilities over all the ten models' predictions. Instances with averaged probability higher than 0.5 are classified as irrelevance and vice versa.

Data Annotation

We invite human editors to label sentences. Instructions for labeling are shown as follows. First, a salient fact sentence should be relevant to the targeted entity, i.e. mentioning at least one attribute/aspect of the entity. The purpose is to exclude irrelevant contents. Second, this attribute or aspect should be novel to readers. The purpose is to reveal unknown information of the entity to readers. Third, the salient fact sentence should use measurable descriptions. The purpose is to avoid subjective opinions that lead to biased understanding of the entity. We leave the understanding of the three conditions to annotators. We select the sentences that satisfy the first condition and meet either the second or third condition as salient facts.

To measure whether the labels are consistent, we randomly sample 100 sentences (i.e. 50 salient facts and 50 normal sentences) from the three domains. We invite two annotators to relabel these sentences and calculate cohen's kappa score as inter-annotator agreement. The score is 0.80 that is comparable to the results of existing helpful reviews annotation, e.g., 0.81 from a SEMEVAL-

[4]We obtain the scores using lm-scorer library (LMScorer, 2018) from Github

[5]https://github.com/huggingface/transformers

Domain	salient	normal
Hotel	complementary wine the rooftop deck Rooftop bar	an experience my stay a few small requests
Product	a thick liner note very computer savvy Win XP	Books this phone system well!2weeks
Restaurant	Ample parking $33.50 The 5 oz	bone marrow toast Excellent hashbrowns Customer service

Table 9: Key phrases extracted from salient facts and normal sentences, respectively. The comparison explains that salient facts reveal finer-grained attributes or quantitative descriptions of an entity that make them specific.

	Hotel	Product	Restaurant
Random guess	0.169	0.076	0.045
`Unique` model	0.395	0.205	0.114
w. Entity name removal	0.412	-	0.109
w. Irrelevance removal	0.401	0.201	0.128
ZL-Distiller	0.407	0.201	0.144

Table 10: Ablation study over Hotel, Product, and Restaurant datasets using ZL-Distiller. F1 of ZL-Distiller increases when turning on individual optimizations. Product has no entity name removal optimization because the dataset has no associated product names in the reviews.

2019 Competition task 9 (Negi and Buitelaar, 2015) and 0.59 from TipRank (Guy et al., 2017b)). The result suggests that annotators have a high degree of agreement on salient facts.

Explanation of Saliency with Key Phrases

To understand what elements in a sentence make it salient, we extract key phrases of salient facts and normal sentences. We search span in a sentence that has the highest weights of BERT attention mechanism as key phrase. We present key phrase samples of salient spans and non-salient spans for Hotel, Product, and Restaurant domains in Table 9.

Salient facts show three patterns. First, the description targeted at attributes of an entity. In Product domain, for example, “thick liner note” or “Win XP” mention a specific product attribute, while “Books” and “well!2weeks” do not link to any attribute. Second, the attributes are novel that go beyond common knowledge. In Hotel domain, for example, “rooftop bar” or “wine” is unusual in hotel entities, compared with “an experience” and “small requests”. Third, the description of an attribute reveals its quantity. In Restaurant domain, for example, “Ample parking” or “$33.50” relate to quantitative descriptions while “excellent hashbrowns” and “Customer service” do not reveal quantitative information of corresponding attributes. The results suggest that the most salient facts are those sentences that quantitatively describe novel attribute(s) of an entity.

Effect of `Unique` Model

We first evaluate the performance of `Unique` model that formulates salient fact extraction problem as entity prediction. Specifically, we randomly sample 10 entities and train a BERT model using reviews from the 10 entities. The total of training instances used for Hotel, Product, and Restaurant is 95,454, 44,560, and 356,505, respectively. The training takes a review to predict its targeted entity. After training, we compute the score for each review sentence using Equation 1. To evaluate the approach, we split data using 5-fold approach where one fold is used for finding the best threshold and the other four folds for testing. A total of five rounds are tested and F1 scores are averaged as the final score.

We report F1 scores of `Unique` model on Hotel, Product, and Restaurant in Table 10. The F1 scores are 0.395, 0.205, and 0.114, respectively. To understand whether the F1 scores are significant, we evaluate the performance of random guess, a baseline that predicts a sentence as salient fact at the probability of $\%Positive$, with $\%Positives$ representing the ratio of positive labels of a dataset (see Table 3). The F1 score of random guess for Hotel, Product, and Restaurant is 0.153, 0.065, and 0.095, respectively and are lower than those of `Unique` model. The results suggest that `Unique` model can effectively improve extraction qualities of random guess, in various domains. Therefore, `Unique` is a strong signal of saliency that can be applied to different domains.

Effect of `Informative` Model

Effect of entity name removal. We evaluate the effect of entity name removal on `Unique` model and report F1 scores in Table 10, with exception for Product. Since the dataset has no associated product names in the reviews, we cannot enable the optimization. On Hotel, the F1 score of `Unique` model increases from 0.395 to 0.412, and the increment is 0.017. However, the F1 score on Restaurant decreases from 0.114 to 0.109. The

Model	Top-n 10	30	50	100
	Hotel			
PacSum (tfidf)	**0.178**	0.308	0.376	0.370
ZL-Distiller +PacSum (tfidf)	0.133	**0.338**	**0.424**	**0.415**
	Product			
PacSum (tfidf)	**0.414**	0.286	0.290	0.218
ZL-Distiller +PacSum (tfidf)	**0.414**	**0.367**	**0.319**	**0.252**
	Restaurant			
PacSum (tfidf)	**0.200**	0.150	0.133	0.109
ZL-Distiller +PacSum (tfidf)	**0.200**	**0.300**	**0.200**	**0.145**

Table 11: Performance of zero-shot learning (i.e. PacSum and ZL-Distiller + PacSum) with zero labels. Best F1 scores are marked in bold.

decrement is 0.005. Overall, removing entity name does more good than harm. The results indicate that entity names overall mislead the `Unique` model and should be removed.

Effect of irrelevance removal. We evaluate the effect of irrelevant sentence removal on `Unique` model and report F1 scores in Table 10. After applying irrelevant sentences removal, the F1 score of `Unique` model on Hotel/Restaurant increases from 0.395/0.114 to 0.401/0.128. The increment is 0.006/0.014. However, the F1 score on Product decreases from 0.205 to 0.201, and the decrement is 0.004. Overall, the gain is higher than loss, so removing irrelevant sentences does more good than harm. The results indicate that irrelevant sentences overall mislead the `Unique` model and should be removed.

Overall effect. We evaluate the overall performance of ZL-Distiller when leveraging both `Unique` model and `Informative` model (i.e. turning on entity name removal and irrelevance removal simultaneously). We show F1 scores in Table 10. Compared with `Unique` model only, ZL-Distiller achieves 0.012 and 0.03 F1 gains on Hotel and Restaurant. Meanwhile, ZL-Distiller shows similar F1 on Product with a difference as small as 0.004. We anticipate ZL-Distiller can perform better on Product when entity names are present in the dataset.

Performance of Jointly Unsupervised Prediction

Since ZL-Distiller captures distributional patterns including "unique" and "informative", we would like to understand whether ZL-Distiller is still helpful to the state-of-the-art unsupervised extractor. For this purpose, we use PacSum (Zheng and Lapata, 2019), a recent extractive summarizer, as the representative unsupervised solution. We first obtain PacSum extraction performance using tfidf as sentence embedder. We next combine PacSum (tfidf) prediction scores with ZL-Distiller prediction scores and denote the combination as ZL-Distiller + PacSum (tfidf). Specifically, ZL-Distiller + PacsuM (tfidf) takes products of PacSum (tfidf) scores and ZL-Distiller scores then ranks sentences by product scores. We take the top-n as the predicted salient facts and vary n with 10, 30, 50, and 100. For each n, the F1 score is reported.

We present the F1 scores of PackSum (tfidf) and ZL-Distiller + PacSum (tfidf) in Table 11. ZL-Distiller + PacSum (tfidf) improves the F1 score of PacSum (tfidf) on 11 out of the 12 settings. Specifically, ZL-Distiller + PacSum (tfidf) outperforms PacSum (tfidf) on Product and Restaurant on all of the top 10, 30, 50, and 100 settings, and on Hotel on top 30, 50, and 100 settings. The results suggest that ZL-Distiller overall is helpful to the state-of-the-art unsupervised solution towards better extraction performance.

Technical Novelty

Herein, we proposed to exploit distributional patterns for review mining tasks. Our results demonstrate that distributional patterns are auxiliary patches to salient fact extraction as they lead to better performance when combined together. Therefore, we expect that the deployment of distributional patterns in relevant studies, such as helpful review prediction or suggestion mining, can also generate better results, which will extensively expand the applications of our proposed pattern in the field of review mining. We also proposed a scoring mechanism that works well on a variety of domains (i.e., hotel, product, restaurant) in both supervised and unsupervised settings. The scoring mechanism together with target_name and irrelevant_sentence_removal models lead to unbiased and unique results in Question Answering and Entity Summarization, compared to the results without their processing. Finding useful reviews is of high practical importance and can be applied to many NLP problems. We chose the most appropriate mechanisms instead of developing new methods to have the best results. In the future, we will apply this task to mining more informative reviews for a variety of NLP domains and applications.

Automatic Fake News Detection: Are current models "fact-checking" or "gut-checking"?

Ian Kelk **Benjamin Basseri** **Wee Yi Lee** **Richard Qiu** **Chris Tanner**

Harvard University
{iak415@g,basseri@cs50,wel390@g}.harvard.edu
{rqiu@college,christanner@g}.harvard.edu

Abstract

Automatic fake news detection models are ostensibly based on logic, where the truth of a claim made in a headline can be determined by supporting or refuting evidence found in a resulting web query. These models are believed to be reasoning in some way; however, it has been shown that these same results, or better, can be achieved without considering the claim at all – only the evidence. This implies that other signals are contained within the examined evidence, and could be based on manipulable factors such as emotion, sentiment, or part-of-speech (POS) frequencies, which are vulnerable to adversarial inputs. We neutralize some of these signals through multiple forms of both neural and non-neural pre-processing and style transfer, and find that this flattening of extraneous indicators can induce the models to actually require both claims and evidence to perform well. We conclude with the construction of a model using emotion vectors built off a lexicon and passed through an "emotional attention" mechanism to appropriately weight certain emotions. We provide quantifiable results that prove our hypothesis that manipulable features are being used for fact-checking.

1 Introduction

Recent events such as the last two U.S. presidential elections have been greatly affected by fake news, defined as "fabricated information that disseminates deceptive content, or grossly distort actual news reports, shared on social media platforms" (Allcott and Gentzkow, 2017). In fact, the World Economic Forum 2013 report designates massive digital misinformation as a major technological and geopolitical risk (Bovet and Makse, 2019). As daily social media usage increases (Statista Research Department, 2021), manual fact-checking cannot keep up with this deluge of information.

Automatic fact-checking models are therefore a necessity, and most of them function using a system of *claims* and *evidence* (Hassan et al., 2017). Given a specific claim, the models use external knowledge as evidence. Typically, a web search query is treated as the claim, and a subset of the top search results is treated as the evidence. There is an implicit assumption that the fact-checking models are reasoning in some way, using the evidence to confirm or refute the claim. Recent research (Hansen et al., 2021) found this conclusion may be premature; current models can show improved performance when considering evidence alone, essentially fact-checking an unasked question. While this might seem reasonable given that the evidence is conditioned on the claims by the search engine, this can be exploited as illustrated in Figure 1, which shows that evidence returned using a ridiculous claim can still appear reasonable if we view the evidence alone without the claim. Furthermore, textual entailment requires both a text and a hypothesis; if we have a result without a hypothesis, we are performing a different, unknown task.

This finding indicates a problem with current automatic fake news detection, signaling that the models rely on features in the evidence typical to fake news, rather than using entailment. Since most automated fact-checking research is primarily concerned with the accuracy of the results, rather than addressing *how* the results are achieved, we propose a novel investigation into these models and their evidence. We use a variety of pre-processing steps, including neural and non-neural ones, to attempt to reduce the affectations common in evidence:

- Stemming, stopword removal, negation, and POS-filtering (Babanejad et al., 2020).
- Style transfer neural models using the *Styleformer* model to perform **informal-to-formal** and **formal-to-informal** paraphrasing methods (Li et al., 2018; Schmidt, 2020).

We also develop our own BERT-based model as an extension of the *EmoCred* system (Giachanou

Proceedings of the Fifth Fact Extraction and VERification Workshop (FEVER), pages 29 - 36
May 26, 2022 ©2022 Association for Computational Linguistics

Figure 1: An example of why evidence alone does not suffice in identifying fake news, despite the evidence being conditioned on the claim as a search-engine query. Although the returned evidence appearing reputable, it is clear that it has little relevance to deciding the veracity of the claim that "all Canadians have eaten at least one bear."

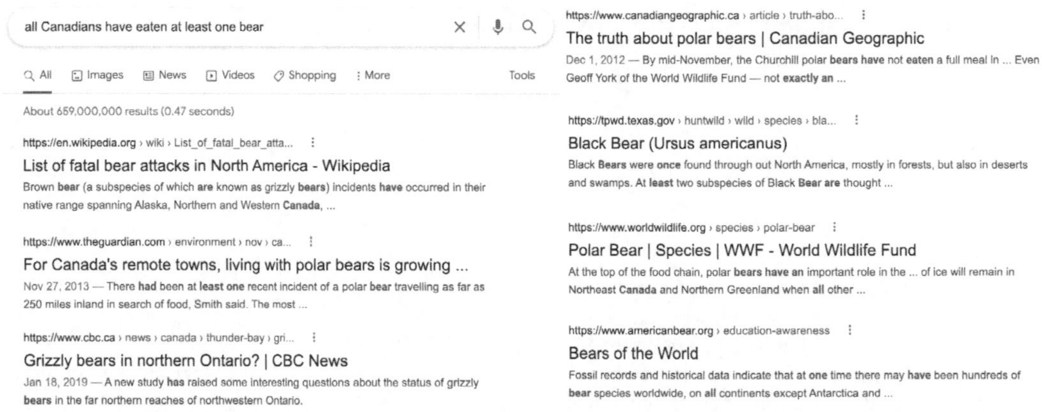

et al., 2019), adding an "emotional attention" layer to weight the most relevant emotional signals in a given evidence snippet. We make our code publicly available. [1]

With each of these methods, we focus on scores where the models perform better using **both the claims and the evidence combined**, $S_{C\&E}$, rather than with the **evidence alone**, S_E. Going forward, we will refer to the difference between these dataset combinations as the $delta$ of the pre-processing step, where $delta = S_{C\&E} - S_E$. A positive $delta$ score indicates that the claim was useful and helped yield an increase in performance. Since we are removing indicators that the current models rely on, some of the models perform *worse* at the task than they did previously. However, a surprising result is that many *improved*, and the need to consider the claim and the evidence together is a sign of using reasoning rather than manipulable indicators.

Under current fact-checking models, adversarial data can subvert these detectors. Paraphrasing can be performed by inserting fictitious statements into otherwise truthful evidence with little effect on the model's output. For example, an article titled "Is the GOP losing Walmart?", could have "Walmart" substituted with "Apple," and the predictions are nearly identical despite the news now being fictitious (Zhou et al., 2019).

[1] GitHub repository link

2 Related Work

There has been significant work with automatic fact-checking models using RNNs and Transformers (Shaar et al., 2020a; Alam et al., 2020; Shaar et al., 2020b) as well as non-neural machine learning using TF-IDF vectors (Reddy et al., 2018).

Current fake news detection models that use a claim's search engine results as evidence may unintentionally use hidden signals that are not attributed to the claim (Hansen et al., 2021). Additionally, models may in fact simply memorize biases within data (Gururangan et al., 2018). Improvements can be made when using human-identified justifications for fact-checking (Alhindi et al., 2018; Vo and Lee, 2020), and making use of textual entailment can offer improvements (Saikh et al., 2019).

Emotional text can signal low credibility (Rashkin et al., 2017), characterizing fake news as a task where pre-processing can be used effectively to diminish bias (Giachanou et al., 2019; Babanejad et al., 2020). A framework to both categorize fake news and to identify features that differentiate fake news from real news has been described by Molina et al. (2021), and debiasing inappropriate subjectivity in text can be accomplished by replacing a single biased word in each sentence (Pryzant et al., 2020).

3 Datasets

We use the MultiFC dataset (Augenstein et al., 2019), which consists of political claims and associated truth labels from PolitiFact and Snopes.

Figure 2: Ablation studies where evidence was sequentially removed for training and evaluation of models. On the far left, we show the most effective non-neural pre-processing compared to the baseline of **none**. Performance generally worsens as the ablation increases.

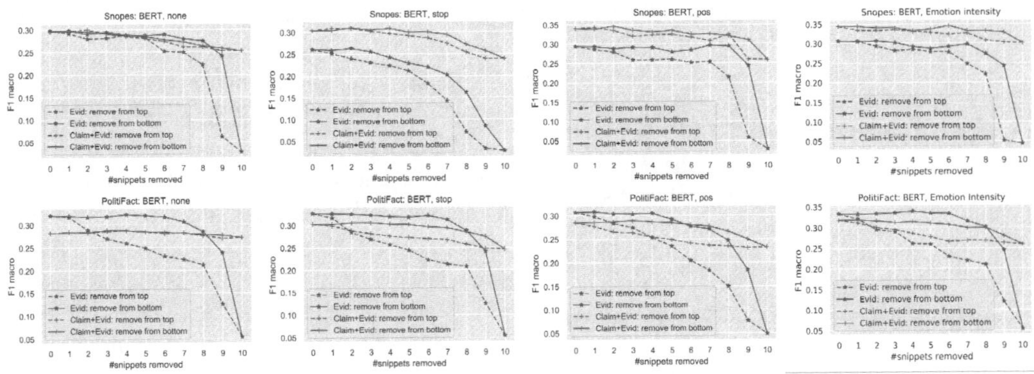

Using the claim as a query, the top ten results from Google News ("snippets") constitute the evidence (Hansen et al., 2021). PolitiFact and Snopes use five labels (False, Mostly False, Mixture, Mostly True, True), which we collapse to True, Mixture, and False.

To construct the emotion vectors for our *EmoAttention* system, we use the NRC Affect Intensity Lexicon, which maps approximately 6,000 terms to values between 0 and 1, representing the term's intensity along 8 different emotions (Mohammad, 2017). For example, "interrupt" and "rage" are both categorized as *anger* words, but with the respective intensity values of 0.333 and 0.911.

4 Models

The most common automatic fact-checking NLP models are based on term frequency, word embeddings, and contextualized word embeddings, using Random Forests, LSTMs, and BERT (Hassan et al., 2017). We limit our experimentation to the BERT model, as it is the highest performing state-of-the-art model and was thoroughly tested in (Hansen et al., 2021). This BERT model with no pre-processing is our baseline model.

For the style transfer model we use the Styleformer model (Li et al., 2018; Schmidt, 2020), a Transformer-based seq2seq model.

We also develop our own BERT-based model using the *EmoLexi* and *EmoInt* implementation of the EmoCred system by adding an *emotional attention layer* to emphasize certain emotion representations for a given claim and its evidence (Giachanou et al., 2019). There is also a *snippet attention layer* attending to which evidence itself should be weighted most heavily for the given claim.

Figure 3: The *EmoAttention* BERT model architecture using *emotional-* and *snippet attention*

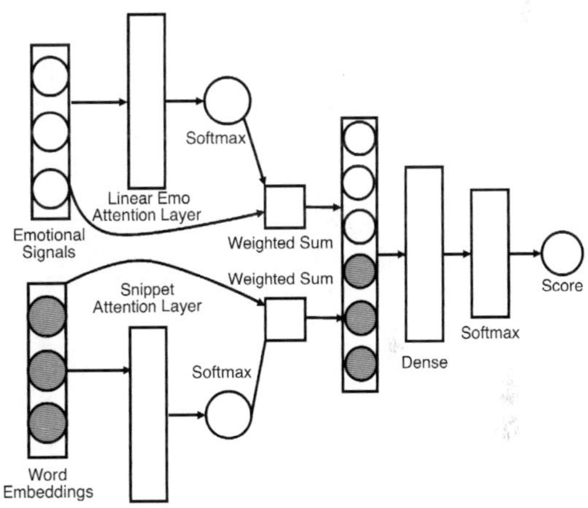

5 Experiments

5.1 Non-neural pre-processing

Our goal is to separate affect-based properties from factual content of the text. Toward this, we run a large number of permutations of the following four simple pre-processing steps (see Figure 4 in Appendix B for results). These steps were chosen as they have been shown to facilitate affective tasks such as sentiment analysis, emotion classification, and sarcasm detection (Babanejad et al., 2020). In some cases we used a modified form — such as removing adverbs for POS pre-processing.

- **Negation (NEG):** A mechanism that transforms a negated statement into its inverse (Benamara et al., 2012). An example, "I am not happy" would have "not" removed and "happy" replaced by its antonym, forming the sentence "I am sad."

- **Parts-of-Speech (POS):** We keep only three parts of speech: nouns, verbs, and adjectives. We initially included adverbs but found removing them improved results. This could be due to some adverbs being emotionally charged.

- **Stopwords (STOP):** These are generally the most common words in a language, such as function words and prepositions. We use the NLTK library.

- **Stemming (STEM):** Reducing a word to its root form. We use the NLTK Snowball Stemmer.

5.2 Neural formality style transfer

We use the adversarial technique of generating paraphrases for all the claims and evidence through style transfer. The neural Transformer-based seq2seq model *Styleformer* changes the formality of the text, and it frequently changes the ordering of the sentence itself, too. For example, the formal-to-informal model changes *"A photograph shows William Harley and Arthur Davidson unveiling their first motorcycle in 1914"* to *"In a 1914 photograph William Harley and Arthur Davidson unveil their first motorcycle."*

As well, it removes punctuation and alters phrasing that might be understood as sarcasm, such as *"Melania Trump said that Native Americans upset about the Dakota Access Pipeline should 'go back to India"'* to *"Melania Trump told Native Americans that was upset by the Dakota Access Pipeline, that they should travel to India."* The informal-to-formal model lowercases everything and also changes the text significantly.

We chose this paraphrasing model based on the idea that fake news – especially that which is frequently posted on social media – has a certain polarizing style that might be neutralized by altering the formality of the text. Rather surprisingly, we received better results transforming the style from formal-to-informal than we did with informal-to-formal.

5.3 EmoCred emotion representations with emotional attention

The *EmoCred* systems of *EmoLexi* and *EmoInt* use a lexicon to determine emotional word counts and intensities, respectively (Giachanou et al., 2019). We use the *NRC Affect Intensity Lexicon*, a "high-coverage lexicons that captures word–affect intensities" for eight basic emotions, which were created using a technique called best–worst scaling (Mohammad, 2017). These eight emotions can be used to create an emotion vector for a sentence, where each index corresponds to a score: [*anger, anticipation, disgust, fear, joy, sadness, surprise, trust*].

As an example, a sentence that contains the word "suffering" conveys *sadness* with an *NRC Affect Intensity Lexicon* intensity of 0.844, whereas the word "affection" indicates *joy* with an intensity of 0.647. We create the vector of length eight, and for each word associated with an emotion, the emotion's indexed value is either: (1) incremented by one for *EmoLexi*; or, (2) incremented by its intensity for *EmoInt*. Thus, the sentence "He had an affection for suffering" would have an *EmoLexi* emotion vector of $[0, 0, 0, 0, 1, 1, 0, 0]$ and an *EmoInt* emotion vector of $[0, 0, 0, 0, 0.647, 0.844, 0, 0]$

We build on this *EmoCred* framework, adding an attention system for emotion that gives a weight to each emotion vector, just as the attention layer for each snippet gives a weight to each snippet. The end result is that two independent attention layers attend to the ten snippets and ten emotional representations independently, and we call the resulting system *Emotional Attention* (see Figure 3).

6 Results

Surprisingly, the four top-performing models with the Snopes dataset include two non-neural models and two neural models. All four achieve greater F1 Macro scores than the baseline BERT model without pre-processing (see Figure 2). POS and STOP yield the biggest delta between $S_{C\&E}$ vs. S_E, followed by *EmoInt* and *Informal Style Transfer*. However, *EmoInt* yields the highest F1 Macro, followed by POS, *Informal*, and STOP.

In PolitiFact, none of the pre-processing steps achieve a delta greater than zero for $S_{C\&E}$ versus S_E. The combination of POS+STOP steps come closest to parity, followed by *EmoInt*, then POS and STOP. For the best F1 Macro scores overall, *EmoAttention*'s two forms (i.e., *EmoInt* and *EmoLexi*) were the two best, followed by STOP

Pre-processing	Snopes $S_{C\&E}$ (Claim+Evidence) F1 Macro	Snopes Δvs S_E (Evidence) F1 Macro	PolitiFact $S_{C\&E}$ (Claim+Evidence) F1 Macro	PolitiFact Δvs S_E (Evidence) F1 Macro
None	0.295	-0.003	0.282	-0.038
POS	0.340	0.046	0.285	-0.022
STOP	0.304	0.043	0.303	-0.023
EmoAttention (EmoInt)	0.344	0.038	0.318	-0.015
EmoAttention (EmoLexi)	0.324	-0.003	0.310	-0.033
POS+STOP	0.312	0.012	0.290	-0.003
Formal to Informal	0.332	0.028	—	—

Table 1: Top results from various pre-processing steps. The top three steps are highlighted in blue. The lowest F1 Macro scores and deltas are in red. With the exception of *EmoLexi* tying for the lowest delta, the best pre-processing steps outperform the baseline BERT model from Hansen et al. (2021).

and POS. All of these pre-processing steps achieve higher F1 Macro scores than the baseline BERT model. Further, they yield better deltas for $S_{C\&E}$ versus S_E, implying that the model now requires the claims to reason.

7 Conclusion

Many pre-processing steps increase both the model's F1 scores and its need for claims *and* evidence, validating our hypothesis that signals in style and tone have become a crutch for fact-checking models. Rather than doing entailment, they are leveraging other signals – perhaps similar to sentiment analysis – and relying on a "gut feeling". *EmoAttention* generates our best predictions and deltas, confirming our suspicion that the models rely on emotionally charged style as a predictive feature. This is further narrowed to emotional *intensity*: the *EmoInt* intensity score-based model performs much better than its count-based counterpart *EmoLexi*. Thus, evidence containing emotions associated with fake news will be considered more when scoring the claim.

One surprising result is the effectiveness of the simple POS and STOP pre-processing steps. POS only included nouns, verbs, and adjectives (i.e., a superset of STOP). This could explain why it has the best delta between $S_{C\&E}$ vs. S_E. Future research could investigate if stopwords, which are often discarded, actually contain signals such as anaphora: a repetitive rhetoric style which can affect NLP analyses (Liddy, 1990).

As an example, Donald Trump makes heavy use of anaphora in his 2017 inauguration speech:

> "Together, **we will** make America strong **again**. **We will** make America wealthy **again**. **We will** make America proud **again**. **We will** make America safe **again**. And, yes, together, **we will** make america great **again**." (Trump Inauguration Address, 2017)

By removing stopwords "we", "will" and "again", the model relies less on the text's rhetoric style and more on the entailment we are seeking. We propose further study on the effects of STOP and POS, as well as experimenting with different emotional vectors and *EmoAttention* to make fact-checking models more robust. Automatic Fake News detection remains a challenging problem, and unfortunately, current fact-checking models can be subverted by adversarial techniques that exploit emotionally charged writing.

A Impact Statement

Disinformation is much more than just a mild inconvenience for society; it has resulted in needless deaths in the COVID-19 pandemic, and has fomented violence and political instability all over the globe (van der Linden et al., 2020). Our goal in this paper is to discover exploitable weaknesses in current fact-checking models and recommend that such models not be relied upon in their current form. We point out how the models are dependent on emotional signals in the texts instead of exclusively performing textual entailment, and that additional research needs to be done to ensure they are performing the proper task.

Harm Minimization Our quantifying of the effects of pre-processing on fact-checking models does not cause any harm to real-world users or companies. Research has demonstrated that adversarial attacks could result in disinformation being labeled as factual news. Disinformation has become increasingly present in global politics, as some nation-states with significant resources have disseminated propaganda to create political dissent in other countries (Zhou et al., 2019). Our research here has demonstrated potential risks: emotional writing could be used as an exploit to circumvent fact-checking models. Thus, we urge others to further illuminate such vulnerabilities, to minimize potential harms, and to encourage improvements with new models.

Deployment Social media companies often deal with fake news by placing highly visible labels. However, simply tagging stories as false can make readers more willing to believe and share *other* false, untagged stories. This unintended consequence – in which the selective labeling of false news makes other news stories seem more legitimate – has been called the "implied-truth effect" (Pennycook et al., 2019). Thus, unless these models become so accurate that they catch *all* fake news presented to them, the entire basis of their use is called into question.

Despite the significant progress in developing models to correctly identify fake news, the real elephant in the room is that many people simply ignore the labels (Molina et al., 2021). There is, however, prior work supporting the idea that if people are warned that a headline is false, they will be less likely to believe it (Ecker et al., 2010; Lewandowsky et al., 2012). Because of this, we believe this research represents a net benefit for humanity.

Warning labels are just one way of dealing with properly identified fake news, and publishers can choose to simply not allow it on their platforms. Of course, this issue leads to questions of censorship.

B Extended Results

In Figure 4, we report all results for each preprocessing step.

References

Firoj Alam, Shaden Shaar, Alex Nikolov, Hamdy Mubarak, Giovanni Da San Martino, Ahmed Abdelali, Fahim Dalvi, Nadir Durrani, Hassan Sajjad, Kareem Darwish, and Preslav Nakov. 2020. Fighting the COVID-19 infodemic: Modeling the perspective of journalists, fact-checkers, social media platforms, policy makers, and the society. *CoRR*, abs/2005.00033.

Tariq Alhindi, Savvas Petridis, and Smaranda Muresan. 2018. Where is your evidence: Improving fact-checking by justification modeling. In *Proceedings of the First Workshop on Fact Extraction and VERification (FEVER)*, pages 85–90, Brussels, Belgium. Association for Computational Linguistics.

Hunt Allcott and Matthew Gentzkow. 2017. Social media and fake news in the 2016 election. *Journal of Economic Perspectives*, 31(2):211–36.

Isabelle Augenstein, Christina Lioma, Dongsheng Wang, Lucas Chaves Lima, Casper Hansen, Christian Hansen, and Jakob Grue Simonsen. 2019. Multifc: A real-world multi-domain dataset for evidence-based fact checking of claims.

Nastaran Babanejad, Ameeta Agrawal, Aijun An, and Manos Papagelis. 2020. A comprehensive analysis of preprocessing for word representation learning in affective tasks. In *Proceedings of the 58th Annual Meeting of the Association for Computational Linguistics*, pages 5799–5810, Online. Association for Computational Linguistics.

Farah Benamara, Baptiste Chardon, Yannick Mathieu, Vladimir Popescu, and Nicholas Asher. 2012. How do negation and modality impact on opinions? In *Proceedings of the Workshop on Extra-Propositional Aspects of Meaning in Computational Linguistics*, ExProM '12, page 10–18, USA. Association for Computational Linguistics.

Alexandre Bovet and Hernán A. Makse. 2019. Influence of fake news in twitter during the 2016 us presidential election. *JournalNature Communications*, 10(1).

Ullrich Ecker, Stephan Lewandowsky, and David Tang. 2010. Explicit warnings reduce but do not eliminate the continued influence of misinformation. *Memory and cognition*, 38:1087–100.

Anastasia Giachanou, Paolo Rosso, and Fabio Crestani. 2019. Leveraging emotional signals for credibility detection. In *Proceedings of the 42nd International ACM SIGIR Conference on Research and Development in Information Retrieval*, SIGIR'19, page 877–880, New York, NY, USA. Association for Computing Machinery.

Suchin Gururangan, Swabha Swayamdipta, Omer Levy, Roy Schwartz, Samuel Bowman, and Noah A. Smith. 2018. Annotation artifacts in natural language inference data. In *Proceedings of the 2018 Conference of the North American Chapter of the Association for Computational Linguistics: Human Language Technologies, Volume 2 (Short Papers)*, pages 107–112, New Orleans, Louisiana. Association for Computational Linguistics.

Casper Hansen, Christian Hansen, and Lucas Chaves Lima. 2021. Automatic fake news detection: Are models learning to reason?

Figure 4: The full table of results for all pre-processing steps for the Snopes (SNES) and PolitiFact (POMT) datasets. Due to the high compute requirements of the formal and informal style transfer models, these datasets were only prepared for the Snopes dataset. The darkest green colors indicate the best results, while the red indicates the worst. Multiple pre-processing steps such as (pos, stop) were performed in the order written.

	Snopes		PolitiFact			Snopes		PolitiFact	
	F1 Micro	F1 Macro	F1 Micro	F1 Macro		F1 Micro	F1 Macro	F1 Micro	F1 Macro
none					pos, stop				
Claim	0.511	0.296	0.269	0.275	Claim	0.552	0.267	0.257	0.264
Evidence	0.556	0.298	0.314	0.320	Evidence	0.551	0.300	0.287	0.293
Claim & Evidence	0.607	0.295	0.278	0.282	Claim & Evidence	0.527	0.312	0.287	0.290
Δ: (Claim & Ev.) - Ev.	0.051	-0.003	-0.036	-0.038	Δ: (Claim & Ev) - Ev.	-0.024	0.012	0.000	-0.003
neg					pos, neg, stop				
Claim	0.545	0.332	0.264	0.272	Claim	0.510	0.278	0.261	0.263
Evidence	0.552	0.322	0.315	0.326	Evidence	0.507	0.308	0.287	0.299
Claim & Evidence	0.537	0.324	0.290	0.298	Claim & Evidence	0.577	0.311	0.249	0.259
Δ: (Claim & Ev) - Ev.	-0.015	0.002	-0.025	-0.028	Δ: (Claim & Ev) - Ev.	0.070	0.003	-0.038	-0.040
stop					claim neutralization				
Claim	0.528	0.273	0.249	0.250	Claim	0.529	0.289	0.272	0.274
Evidence	0.521	0.261	0.317	0.326	Evidence	0.538	0.315	0.333	0.343
Claim & Evidence	0.519	0.304	0.296	0.303	Claim & Evidence	0.586	0.304	0.287	0.290
Δ: (Claim & Ev) - Ev.	-0.002	0.043	-0.021	-0.023	Δ: (Claim & Ev) - Ev.	0.048	-0.011	-0.046	-0.053
pos					emo-int				
Claim	0.534	0.292	0.266	0.268	Claim	0.542	0.298	0.271	0.280
Evidence	0.576	0.294	0.295	0.307	Evidence	0.586	0.306	0.323	0.333
Claim & Evidence	0.590	0.340	0.275	0.285	Claim & Evidence	0.582	0.344	0.310	0.318
Δ: (Claim & Ev) - Ev.	0.014	0.046	-0.020	-0.022	Δ: (Claim & Ev) - Ev.	-0.004	0.038	-0.013	-0.015
stem					emo-lexi				
Claim	0.568	0.276	0.258	0.264	Claim	0.517	0.319	0.269	0.276
Evidence	0.588	0.294	0.322	0.329	Evidence	0.516	0.327	0.342	0.343
Claim & Evidence	0.451	0.286	0.280	0.283	Claim & Evidence	0.519	0.324	0.302	0.310
Δ: (Claim & Ev) - Ev.	-0.137	-0.008	-0.042	-0.046	Δ: (Claim & Ev) - Ev.	0.003	-0.003	-0.040	-0.033
all					formal				
Claim	0.546	0.322	0.234	0.236	Claim	0.458	0.297	-	-
Evidence	0.557	0.300	0.287	0.295	Evidence	0.520	0.312	-	-
Claim & Evidence	0.542	0.289	0.259	0.263	Claim & Evidence	0.482	0.285	-	-
Δ: (Claim & Ev) - Ev.	-0.015	-0.011	-0.028	-0.032	Δ: (Claim & Ev) - Ev.	-0.038	-0.027		
pos, neg					informal				
Claim	0.510	0.278	0.266	0.268	Claim	0.536	0.298	-	-
Evidence	0.526	0.299	0.295	0.307	Evidence	0.537	0.304	-	-
Claim & Evidence	0.577	0.311	0.275	0.285	Claim & Evidence	0.611	0.332	-	-
Δ: (Claim & Ev) - Ev.	0.051	0.012	-0.020	-0.022	Δ: (Claim & Ev) - Ev.	0.074	0.028		

Naeemul Hassan, Fatma Arslan, Chengkai Li, and Mark Tremayne. 2017. Toward automated fact-checking: Detecting check-worthy factual claims by claimbuster. In *Proceedings of the 23rd ACM SIGKDD International Conference on Knowledge Discovery and Data Mining*, KDD '17, page 1803–1812, New York, NY, USA. Association for Computing Machinery.

Stephan Lewandowsky, Ullrich K. H. Ecker, Colleen M. Seifert, Norbert Schwarz, and John Cook. 2012. Misinformation and its correction: Continued influence and successful debiasing. *Psychological Science in the Public Interest*, 13(3):106–131. PMID: 26173286.

Juncen Li, Robin Jia, He He, and Percy Liang. 2018. Delete, retrieve, generate: A simple approach to sentiment and style transfer. *CoRR*, abs/1804.06437.

Elizabeth DuRoss Liddy. 1990. Anaphora in natural language processing and information retrieval. *Information Processing & Management*, 26(1):39–52. Special Issue: Natural Language Processing and Information Retrieval.

Saif M. Mohammad. 2017. Word affect intensities. *CoRR*, abs/1704.08798.

Maria D. Molina, S. Shyam Sundar, Thai Le, and Dongwon Lee. 2021. "fake news" is not simply false information: A concept explication and taxonomy of online content. *American Behavioral Scientist*, 65(2):180–212.

Gordon Pennycook, Adam Bear, and Evan Collins. 2019. The implied truth effect: Attaching warnings to a subset of fake news headlines increases perceived accuracy of headlines without warnings. *Management Science*, page 1.

Reid Pryzant, Richard Martinez, Nathan Dass, Sadao Kurohashi, Dan Jurafsky, and Diyi Yang. 2020. Automatically neutralizing subjective bias in text. *Proceedings of the AAAI Conference on Artificial Intelligence*, 34:480–489.

Hannah Rashkin, Eunsol Choi, Jin Yea Jang, Svitlana Volkova, and Yejin Choi. 2017. Truth of varying shades: Analyzing language in fake news and political fact-checking. In *Proceedings of the 2017 Conference on Empirical Methods in Natural Language Processing*, pages 2931–2937, Copenhagen, Denmark. Association for Computational Linguistics.

Aniketh Janardhan Reddy, Gil Rocha, and Diego Esteves. 2018. Defactonlp: Fact verification using entity recognition, TFIDF vector comparison and decomposable attention. *CoRR*, abs/1809.00509.

Tanik Saikh, Amit Anand, Asif Ekbal, and Pushpak Bhattacharyya. 2019. *A Novel Approach Towards Fake News Detection: Deep Learning Augmented with Textual Entailment Features*, pages 345–358.

Robert Schmidt. 2020. Generative text style transfer for improved language sophistication. Stanford CS230.

Shaden Shaar, Giovanni Da San Martino, Nikolay Babulkov, and Preslav Nakov. 2020a. That is a known lie: Detecting previously fact-checked claims. *CoRR*, abs/2005.06058.

Shaden Shaar, Alex Nikolov, Nikolay Babulkov, Firoj Alam, Alberto Barrón-Cedeño, Tamer Elsayed, Maram Hasanain, Reem Suwaileh, Fatima Haouari, Giovanni Da San Martino, and Preslav Nakov. 2020b. Overview of checkthat! 2020 english: Automatic identification and verification of claims in social media. In *CLEF*.

Sander van der Linden, Jon Roozenbeek, and Josh Compton. 2020. Inoculating against fake news about covid-19. *Frontiers in Psychology*, 11:2928.

Nguyen Vo and Kyumin Lee. 2020. Where are the facts? searching for fact-checked information to alleviate the spread of fake news. In *Proceedings of the 2020 Conference on Empirical Methods in Natural Language Processing (EMNLP)*, pages 7717–7731, Online. Association for Computational Linguistics.

Zhixuan Zhou, Huankang Guan, Meghana Moorthy Bhat, and Justin Hsu. 2019. Fake news detection via NLP is vulnerable to adversarial attacks. *CoRR*, abs/1901.09657.

A Semantics-Aware Approach to Automated Claim Verification

Blanca Calvo Figueras
Barcelona Supercomputing Center
blanca.calvo@bsc.es

Montse Cuadros
Vicomtech Foundation, Basque Research and Technology Alliance (BRTA)
mcuadros@vicomtech.org

Rodrigo Agerri
HiTZ Center - Ixa, University of the Basque Country UPV/EHU
rodrigo.agerri@ehu.eus

Abstract

The influence of fake news in the perception of reality has become a mainstream topic in the last years due to the fast propagation of misleading information. In order to help in the fight against misinformation, automated solutions to fact-checking are being actively developed within the research community. In this context, the task of Automated Claim Verification is defined as assessing the truthfulness of a claim by finding evidence about its veracity. In this work we empirically demonstrate that enriching a BERT model with explicit semantic information such as Semantic Role Labelling helps to improve results in claim verification as proposed by the FEVER benchmark. Furthermore, we perform a number of explainability tests that suggest that the semantically-enriched model is better at handling complex cases, such as those including passive forms or multiple propositions.

1 Introduction

With the rise of digital channels that disseminate all kinds of information, misinformation has become a big challenge for a healthy society (Hermida, 2010). Fake news has been defined as a news article or message published through media that carries false information (Kshetri and Voas, 2017). Although this is not a new phenomenon, the current absence of control systems in social media facilitates the fast spreading of misinformation, arriving to a large number of users and greatly influencing their perception of real world events (Zubiaga et al., 2018). Recent work has shown that fake news spread faster in social media than factual news (Vosoughi et al., 2018), which is why researchers from different fields have proposed using automated solutions to help dealing with this situation (Zhou and Zafarani, 2020; Oshikawa et al., 2020).

Claim verification is the task of assessing the veracity of a statement by finding evidence about the claimed facts. This work is usually done manually by fact-checkers, who use their trusted sources to label the claims as true, false or other assessments. Automated Claim Verification, as proposed by Thorne et al. (2018), consists in, given a claim, finding the evidence regarding the veracity of that claim to then infer its truth-label. Systems for Automated Claim Verification have been trained both using synthetic data (Thorne et al., 2018; Jiang et al., 2020), and crawling datasets from fact-checking websites (Augenstein et al., 2019; Wang, 2017). These datasets have enabled the development of models for the three tasks involved in the claim-verification pipeline: document retrieval (Chen et al., 2017a; Nogueira and Cho, 2020), sentence retrieval (Danesh et al., 2015; Hanselowski et al., 2018), and natural language inference (Parikh et al., 2016; Chen et al., 2017b). In this work, we focus on the last module: natural language inference (NLI).

Given the right pieces of evidence, a fact-checking system will have to reason over all the utterances involved in order to determine if the claim can be supported, refuted, or whether there is not enough info to do so. In Figure 1, for instance, it should recognize that the *Rodney King riots* is the same entity in the claim and in evidence 1. Then, it should identify that the location of this event is *Los Angeles County*, and understand that evidence 2 confirms that this happens to be *the most populous county in the USA*.

As illustrated in Figure 1, this reasoning process requires a deep understanding of the semantics of all the utterances involved. In this work, we propose to introduce explicit semantic knowledge in order to improve the systems for Automated Claim Verification. We hypothesize that this information might guide the natural language inference model in claims that have complex semantics.

The linguistic information we use in this work is Semantic Role Labelling (SRL, Palmer et al., 2005) and Open Information Extraction (OpenIE,

Proceedings of the Fifth Fact Extraction and VERification Workshop (FEVER), pages 37 - 48
May 26, 2022 ©2022 Association for Computational Linguistics

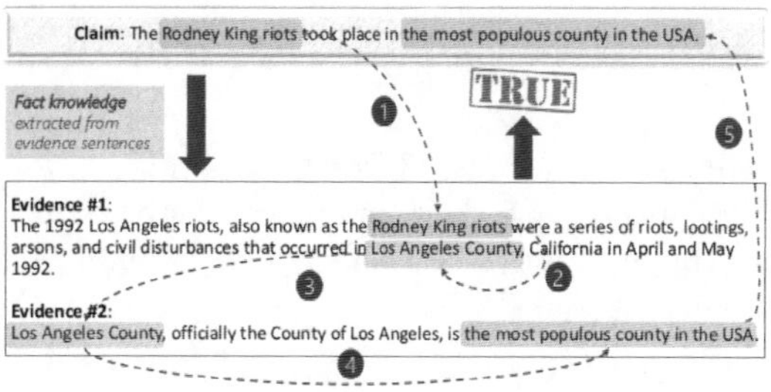

Figure 1: Natural language inference reasoning example, by Zhong et al. (2020)

Etzioni et al., 2008). In our experiments, these semantic structures are used as additional input to the BERT contextualized word embeddings (Devlin et al., 2019). We integrate this information using the SemBERT architecture presented in Zhang et al. (2020a).
The contributions of this work are the following:

- We perform a qualitative analysis to compare synthetic datasets and naturally-occurring datasets for claim verification. We find that synthetic claims are semantically more simple.

- We improve the widely used BERT language model to address the inferential component of the task by adding explicit semantic information. We also make publicly available our model to the community.

- We perform explainability tests to understand the influence of the additional semantic information. The performed tests suggest that the semantically-enriched model is better at handling complex cases.

In the following sections, we introduce previous work on datasets, systems and semantic structures (Section 2), we explain our experiments (Section 3) and expose the primary results (Section 4), we perform explainability tests to qualitatively assess the influence of semantic structures (Section 5), and finally we draw our conclusions and future work (Section 6).

2 Related Work

Automated Claim Verification is a relatively new task, and a lot of effort have been put on how to develop datasets to train automated systems for this task. In the following subsections we introduce some of these efforts and the systems that have been developed on these datasets. We also present previous work using semantic structures.

2.1 Datasets

Ideally, a claim verification system should be able to take sentences from naturally-occurring texts (e.g. news articles, social media posts or political speeches) and assess their veracity. However, developing training data for this task has some complexities, such as defining the ground truth and creating a knowledge database with boundaries, which allows the annotators to know for sure that the ground truth is right. For this reason, there have been several attempts to approximate the task by creating domain-specific datasets (Scifact, Wadden et al., 2020) and synthetic datasets (FEVER and HoVer, Thorne et al., 2018; Jiang et al., 2020). These datasets consist of a set of claims annotated with their ground truth, together with a knowledge base, in which the truth labels are based (e.g. a set of scientific abstracts or a set of Wikipedia articles). The labels are usually Supports, Refutes and NotEnoughInfo. Due to its size and popularity, FEVER has become a benchmark for Automated Claim Verification and has been used in the organization of several shared tasks.

Other datasets exist containing naturally-occurring claims (Augenstein et al., 2019; Wang, 2017). These are generally scraped from fact-checking websites, and sometimes include the justification of the fact-checker for the given label. However, these datasets do not contain a fixed database of evidence. This makes it very difficult to use them to train inference systems, as the ground truth at the moment of fact-checking can be different from the current one. Additionally, there is a high heterogeneity in the inventory of labels across different fact-checking platforms.

2.2 Systems

In the first FEVER shared task (2018), Nie et al. (2019) obtained the highest label accuracy by adding the sentence similarity score between claim and evidence to the embedding representation of evidences. Hanselowski et al. (2018) (UKP-Athene) won the task by using noun phrases to query the Wikipedia search API in the retrieval module.

After the shared task, better results were achieved using transformer-based models (Soleimani et al., 2019). Further improvements came from rethinking the interaction between the pieces of evidences. Zhou et al. (2019) (GEAR) developed a graph approach that uses an attention layer to propagate the information within the evidences. And Zhong et al. (2020) (DREAM) used semantic information to break the evidences into arguments, which then interacted with each other in a graph approach. These two last approaches both used transformer-based models and helped to advance the state-of-the-art on this task. Finally, a recent work (Krishna et al., 2021) developed a system (ProoFVer) based on sequences of natural language logic relations, where the proofs are generated from the claims and corresponding evidence by a seq2seq model (Lewis et al., 2020) and represented as triples. The last inferential step is performed using natural logic proofs only. ProoFVer is the current state-of-the-art on the FEVER benchmark.

Finally, Augenstein et al. (2019) developed a multi-task learning system to deal with a dataset of naturally-occurring claims. They accounted for the multiple labels by creating embeddings for each of these labels, and combining those with the evidence-claim embedding.

2.3 Semantic Structures

Natural Language Inference can be framed as a relation extraction task: in order to know if a sentence is entailed by another sentence, it is necessary to identify the semantic relation between the verb and the arguments of both the premises and hypothesis. For this reason, early approaches used semantic information to approach tasks that required NLI. He et al. (2015) introduced the possibility of annotating semantic roles as a question-answering task, showing that predicate-argument structures can be extracted from natural language questions. In the same direction, Stanovsky et al. (2015) demonstrated the contribution of semantic structures, such as OpenIE, when performing text comprehension with a simple unsupervised lexical matching algorithm.

The creation of more extensive datasets (Bowman et al., 2015; Williams et al., 2018) enabled the development of systems based on neural networks (Wang and Jiang, 2016). Later, the release of transformer-based language models (Devlin et al., 2019; Liu et al., 2019; Yang et al., 2019) revolutionized the performance of many NLP tasks, which also was reflected in NLI.

Recently, a new research direction has suggested using information that had been helpful for NLI models before the arrival of deep learning, in order to guide the self-attention mechanisms (Zhang et al., 2020b). Zanzotto et al. (2020) designed a system that explicitly embeds syntax parse trees into sentence embeddings using distributed tree kernels, and can visualise the decisions made (KERMIT). Zhang et al. (2020a) introduced a modified BERT architecture (SemBERT), that maps semantic role labels (SRL) to embeddings in parallel and integrates the text representation with the contextual explicit semantic embedding to obtain a joint representation. In automated claim verification, Zhong et al. (2020) used SRL tuples to structure information graphs.

A variety of lexical resources have been developed to structure the semantics of sentences with different focus (Baker et al., 1998; Kipper et al., 2000). Semantic roles (SRL), for instance, represent the different arguments that a predicate might have. These semantic categories are relations between noun phrases and verbs. An ideal set of roles should be able to concisely label the arguments of any relation. Nonetheless, the exact set of these relations remains an open discussion inside the linguistic community (Bonial et al., 2011).

SRL in PropBank (Palmer et al., 2005) was designed to be used in automated tasks. The goal of this framework is to create a shallow but broad representation that covers every instance of every verb in a corpus to allow representative statistics to be calculated. PropBank defines semantic roles on a verb-by-verb basis: individual verb's semantic arguments are numbered, beginning with zero. In the example in Figure 2, the agent of the verb *bought* is Arg0, the theme is Arg1, the location Arg2, and the price Arg3.

[Mr. Bean]$_{Arg0}$ [bought]$_{V}$ [the sweater]$_{Arg1}$ [from the second hand store]$_{Arg2}$ [for 400 pounds]$_{Arg3}$.

Figure 2: PropBank semantic roles example

Open Information Extraction (OpenIE) was first introduced as an extraction paradigm to tackle an unbounded number of relations (Etzioni et al., 2008). Systems based on OpenIE extract relational tuples from text by identifying relation phrases and the arguments associated to these relations (Mausam et al., 2012). Stanovsky et al. (2015) were the first to propose this task as an intermediate structure for other semantic tasks, similar to what was already being done with other linguistic

	Supports	Refutes	NEI
Training	80,035	29,775	35,639
Development	3,333	3,333	3,333
Test	3,333	3,333	3,333

Table 1: Number of claims in the FEVER dataset

information, such as semantic roles, syntactic dependencies or lexical representations. An example of the difference between SRL in PropBank and OpenIE is shown in Figure 3.

PropBank:

[John]$_{Arg0}$ [refused]$_V$ [to visit a Vegas casino]$_{Arg1}$
[John]$_{Arg0}$ refused to [visit]$_V$ [a Vegas casino]$_{Arg1}$

OpenIE:

[John]$_{Arg}$ [refused to visit]$_V$ [a Vegas casino]$_{Arg}$

Figure 3: Example of the representations extracted with OpenIE and SRL in PropBank from Stanovsky et al. (2015)

3 Experiments

In this work, we use the FEVER dataset (Thorne et al., 2018). We first develop a baseline using the BERT model (Devlin et al., 2019), and then introduce two types of semantic information to the model (SRL and OpenIE) by using the SemBERT architecture (Zhang et al., 2020a).

3.1 Data

The FEVER dataset consists of 185,445 generated claims with its truth label and the evidence for that label, divided between a train, a development and a test set. The statistics can be seen in Table 1.

The claims were generated manually by annotators, using the June 2017 Wikipedia dump. They were given sentences at random and were asked to generate variations of the claims, altering them in ways that may or may not change their truth label. The types of mutations were: paraphrasing, negation, substitution of entity/relation, and making the claim more general or specific. In a second phase, these claims were labelled as Supports, Refutes or NotEnoughInfo (NEI), and the evidences used for the labelling were recorded (Thorne et al., 2018).

FEVER has been criticized for missing some of the complexity that naturally-occurring claims have, such as claims that contain rich semantics in long and complex sentences (Thorne and Vlachos, 2019). For this reason, we decided to perform a

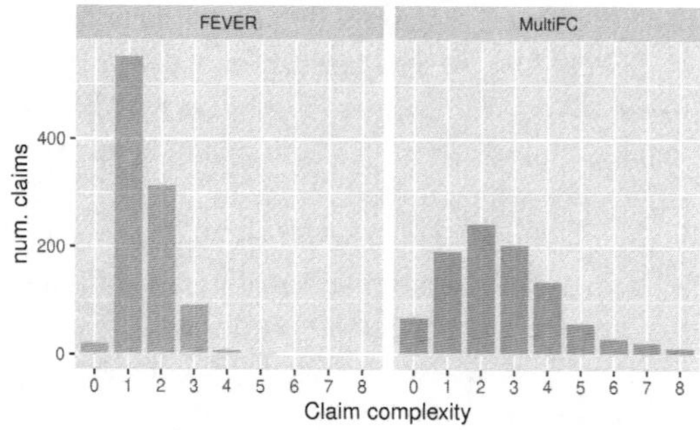

Figure 4: Comparison of claim complexity between FEVER and MultiFC. Axis x indicates the number of verbs per claim.

comparison between the claims in FEVER and in a naturally-occurring claims dataset (MultiFC, Augenstein et al., 2019), we used a sample of 1000 claims of each dataset. As a proxy to measure semantic complexity, we counted the number of verbs per claim[1]. As can be observed in Figure 4, while claims in FEVER are almost always simple (contain 1-2 verbs), MultiFC follows a Benford distribution, in which the number of claims decreases when complexity increases.

This complexity difference lead our attention towards building a system that improves the performance of the semantically complex examples present in FEVER, in order to be able to use these systems in naturally-occurring data.

3.2 Experimental setup

As this work focuses on the NLI module of claim verification, we do not perform evidence retrieval, and instead, we use the evidences retrieved by the system that had the highest evidence recall in the FEVER shared task (Hanselowski et al., 2018). We take the top 5 evidences for each claim.

Given that transformer-based architectures, such as BERT (Devlin et al., 2019), have given state-of-the-art results in the task of NLI (Soleimani et al., 2019), we use this architecture as our baseline, and add the semantic information to it. BERT is designed to be given plain natural text as input. However, recent work suggests that it could benefit from additional linguistic knowledge (Zanzotto et al., 2020; Zhong et al., 2020). Zhang et al. (2020a) proposed an architecture that is able to encode both natural text and semantic information: SemBERT.

[1]Measured with the Universal pos-tags of the nltk package.

At a first step, SemBERT encodes text in the same way that BERT does: tokenizing the text into sub-tokens and computing contextualized embeddings for each of these sub-tokens. In parallel, SemBERT takes the semantic representation that it is given, which should have one tag per word (SRL tags in the original paper), and computes tag embeddings. Given that a single sentence can have several predicates, and consequently several argument-predicate structures (propositions), Zhang et al. (2020a) allow for up to three different representation vectors. A linear layer aggregates the three semantic representation vectors (for the three propositions per sentence allowed) into one final semantic embedding. Then, the BERT word representation and the final semantic representation are concatenated. According to the authors, SemBERT outperforms BERT in NLI tasks, increasing the final accuracy between 1 and 3 percentage points (Zhang et al., 2020a).

In this work, we adapt SemBERT to fit the requirements of Automated Claim Verification. Since we use 5 pieces of evidence per claim, the input to the model consists of 6 sentences. Given that we can have many propositions per instance, we allow up to 12 propositions per instance and implement different sets of tags. Both the SRL tags and the OpenIE tags are extracted with the AllenNLP toolkit (Gardner et al., 2018; Shi and Lin, 2019; Stanovsky et al., 2018) and mapped to the different sets.
To summarise, the model has two separate inputs of the exact same length:

1. The claim plus the 5 concatenated evidences (given to the model as represented in the left part of Figure 5).

2. The semantic tags for each word in the claim and evidences (given to the model as represented in the right part of Figure 5).

Our experiments include a BERT baseline and 5 other models that interact with different sets of semantic tags. All the models have a maximum input length of 250 tokens, and are trained for 4 epochs with a batch size of 20, an AdamW optimizer (Loshchilov and Hutter, 2019) with the learning rate set to 2e-5, and a linear scheduler.

SemBERT_base On first instance, we train a model with all the semantic roles (from now on we will call them tags) retrieved by the AllenNLP parser. This results in a tags-vocabulary of size 19, so the encoding layer contains 19 contextualized embeddings (plus 3 BERT-special tokens) of length 10 (see the tags in Appendix A).

Provided that the set of tags is quite large, the sparsity of the SRL data could be preventing the model from learning patterns. We make additional experiments reducing the set of tags by doing two different mappings.

SemBERT_tags1 One mapping reduces the amount of tags by removing the positional part of the tags, which is given in BIO notation (e.g. I- B-), and reducing the amount of modifier arguments to just *temporal*, *location* or *other modifiers*, leaving a total of 10 tags. The correspondence with the tags of the first model are in Appendix A.

SemBERT_DREAM The second tag set comes from using the mapping of the DREAM system (Zhong et al., 2020), which additionally reduces all the ARG tags to a single *argument* tag, leaving a total of 5 tags. The correspondence can be seen in Appendix A.

SemBERT_Attention The original SemBERT model uses a linear layer to squeeze all the 12 predicates into one. That is needed to remove the multiple predicates dimension and be able to concatenate the representation coming from the SRL to the one produced by BERT. We hypothesized that this linear layer could be replaced by an attention mechanism that allowed evidences to reason between them, inspired by the self-attention mechanism from Zhou et al. (2019).

This self-attention mechanism concatenates the vectors of each predicate in pairs, to then compute self-attention between them and use that information to reshape the 12 representations into one, using a linear layer. To train this model, we used the mapping of SemBERT_tags1.

SemBERT_OpenIE In order to get the OpenIE tags we have also used the AllenNLP parser (Gardner et al., 2018). Then, we have kept the tags *argument*, *verb* and $O - O$ meaning that the word is not part of the predicate. This makes a tag vocabulary of size 3.

4 Results

Table 2 reports the accuracy of the predictions of all these models in the development set. We observe that all the SemBERT experiments have a

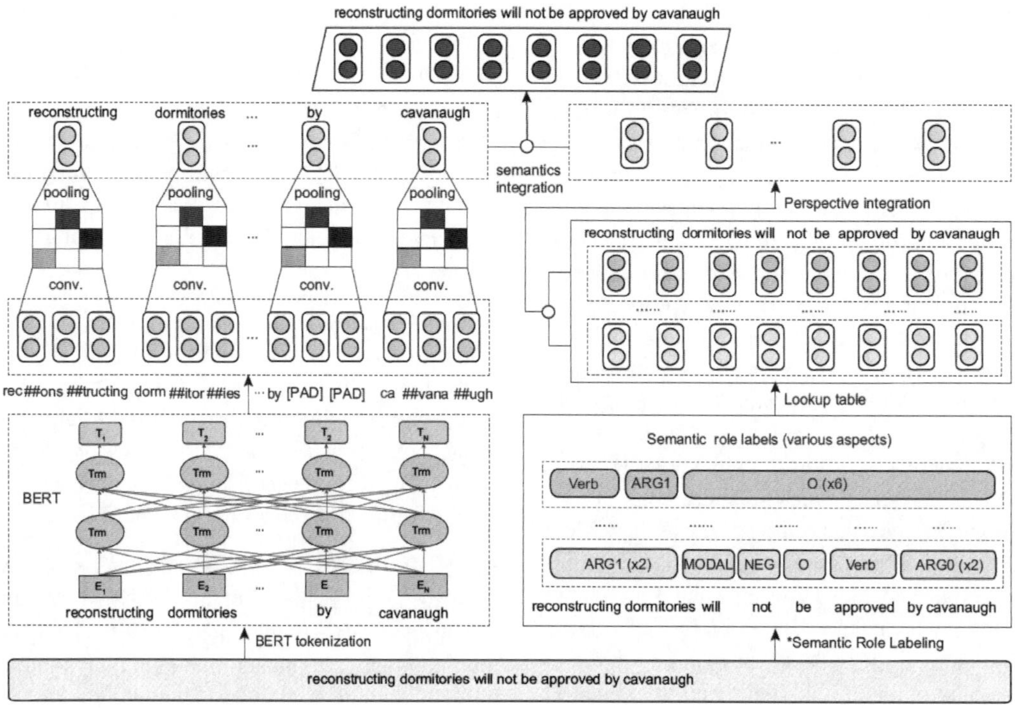

Figure 5: SemBERT architecture by Zhang et al. (2020a)

better performance than the BERT baseline. This difference is of 1 to 2 percentage points. Our best model is the SemBERT model with the SRL set tags1 (SemBERT_tags1).

Going back to our hypothesis that claim complexity will be better understood by using models that include SRL, we calculate the accuracy separately for claims with more (and with less) than 5 verbs. The SemBERT_tags1 model improves 6.5 points on complex claims over BERT, while it just improves 1.5 points on simple claims. However, since FEVER has few complex claims (only 62), further experiments with more complex claims should be used to confirm our hypothesis.

	Label Accuracy
BERT_base (baseline)	73.82
SemBERT_base	75.06
SemBERT_tags1	**75.37**
SemBERT_DREAM	75.12
SemBERT_Attention	74.92
SemBERT_OpenIE	74.34

Table 2: Results from all the models in the FEVER development set

The evaluations on the test set can be seen in

	Evidence F1	**Label Acc.**	**Fever Score**
UKP-Athene	36.97	65.46	61.58
GEAR	36.87	71.60	67.10
DREAM	39.45	76.85	70.60
ProoFVer	40.03	79.47	76.82
BERT_base	36.87	70.86	65.52
SemBERT_tags1	36.87	**72.18**	67.16

Table 3: Results on the test set of our models and previous work

Table 3. In the unseen data, the SemBERT model also outperforms the BERT baseline by 1.3 percentage points in label accuracy. Both models drop around 3 percentage points with respect to the development set. Additionally, we also report the results on the test set of previous work such as UKP-Athene (Hanselowski et al., 2018), GEAR (Zhou et al., 2019), DREAM (Zhong et al., 2020), and ProoFVer (Krishna et al., 2021). For our model, we used the evidences extracted by UKP-Athene, and some pre-processing scripts from GEAR, which explains why all three models have (almost) the same F1 for evidence retrieval. Our model outperforms both of these models in the inference module.

Our approach is similar to the one in DREAM, as both integrate semantic information to improve the reasoning process. However, instead of using a graph-based approach, we use the SemBERT architecture to incorporate the semantic information. As observed, DREAM performs better than our model, suggesting that graph-based architectures might be a better representation for semantic information. Finally, the highest scoring system is ProoFVer[2]. Furthermore, both DREAM and ProoFVer rely on better evidences, as shown by the F1 in Table 3. Still, while being substantially simpler than a higher-performing work such as ProoFVer, our approach provides an effective method to integrate explicit semantic information with clear benefits in performance. Furthermore, our code and model are publicly available to facilitate research on claim verification and reproducibility of results.

5 Explainability tests

While the accuracy results allow for a comparison between models, they are not enough to understand the contribution of the semantic information to the model. For this reason, we decided to perform qualitative explainability tests based on calculating saliency scores and performing adversarial attacks.

5.1 Saliency Scores

Extracting the saliency of each of the tokens given as input is not a trivial task for deep-learning models. Simonyan et al. (2014) proposed to compute them as the gradient of the output with respect to each input. Later improvements to this technique proposed to then multiply these gradients to the input (*InputX-Gradient*), or to overwrite the gradients of the ReLU functions in order to prevent negative gradients from being propagated (*Guided Backpropagation*, Kindermans et al., 2016; Springenberg et al., 2015).

We will use the saliency scores proposed above to get a better grasp of where the model focuses in order to make its inference decisions. For an interpretable output, we want to have one saliency value for each token. Given that the last layer that we can compute the gradients for is the embedding layer, we will get one gradient for each value in the embedding of each token. In order to aggregate these values and get one single value per token we will use the L2 norm (Atanasova et al., 2020).

[2]Results are those reported in the official FEVER leaderboard, which differ from the performance reported in the paper Krishna et al. (2021)

In Figure 6, we can see an example where both BERT and SemBERT get the output right. The instance looks like:

- **Claim**: Telemundo is an English-language television network.
- **Evidence**: Telemundo is an American Spanish-language terrestrial television network owned by Comcast through the NBCUniversal division NBCUniversal Telemundo Enterprises.

Both models output REFUTES and the saliency scores clearly point towards the words *English-language* in the claim, and *Spanish-language* in the evidence. As an opposite case we display Figure 7. In this case, the instance looks like:

- **Claim**: Easy A is directed by Bert V. Royal.
- **Evidence**: Easy A, stylized as easy A, is a 2010 American teen comedy film directed by Will Gluck, written by Bert V. Royal and starring Emma Stone, Stanley Tucci, Patricia Clarkson, Thomas Haden Church, Dan Byrd, Amanda Bynes, Penn Badgley, Cam Gigandet, Lisa Kudrow and Aly Michalka.

In this instance, BERT gets the inference wrong and outputs SUPPORTS, while SemBERT gets it right and outputs REFUTES. Based on the saliency scores, BERT tries to focus on many different tokens, while SemBERT ignores almost all of them. From this observation, we hypothesize that, with such a semantically-complicated evidence (it contains 5 predicates), SemBERT is relying on the semantic information for its decision, which is not plotted on this figure. We further investigate this hypothesis by creating manual adversarial attacks in the next section.

5.2 Adversarial Attacks

Performing adversarial attacks consists on changing the input in order to assess the influence that it has over the output. This has been done both by removing input tokens systematically (Zeiler and Fergus, 2014), and by altering the input instances to generate adversarial attacks which can show what the model actually understands (Ribeiro et al., 2018; Ebrahimi et al., 2018). In this section, we are going to create some manual adversarial attacks in order to test the capabilities of our models.

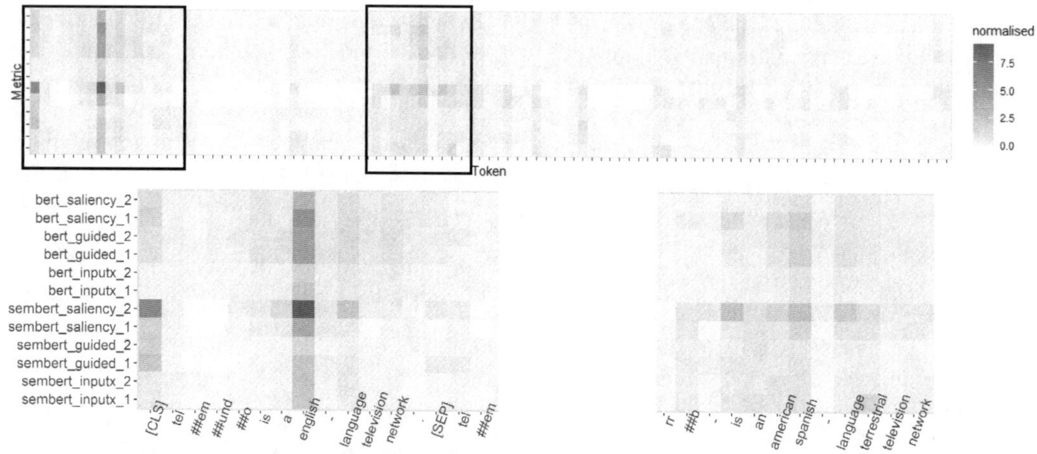

Figure 6: Saliency Scores of the *Telemundo* example with BERT and SemBERT. The above plot shows the entire claim and evidence input, and the plots under it zoom into the relevant parts, delimited with black frames above.

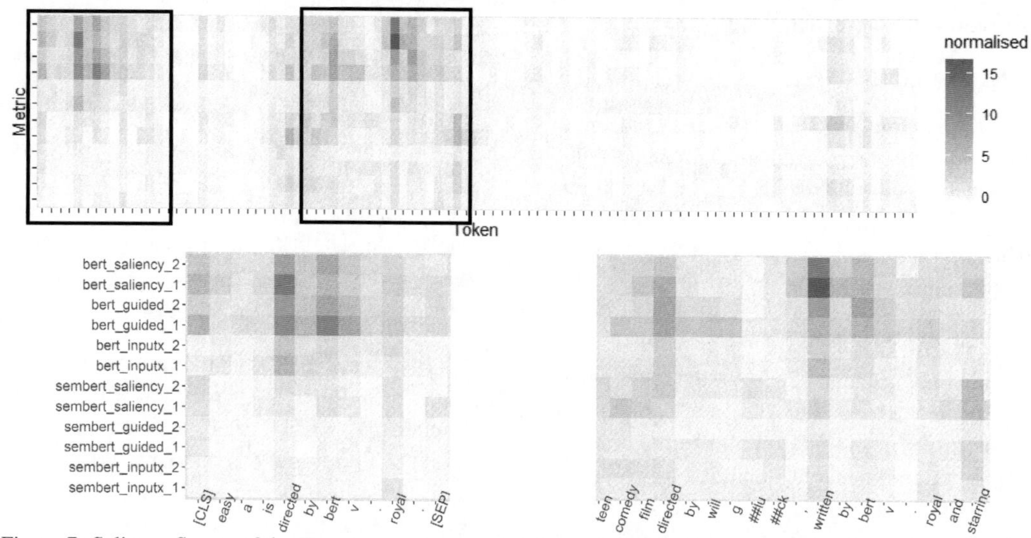

Figure 7: Saliency Scores of the *Easy A* example with BERT and SemBERT. The above plot shows the entire claim and evidence input, and the plots under it zoom into the relevant parts, delimited with black frames above.

Taking the example of *Easy A*, we start by checking that the REFUTES label of SemBERT is not random by changing the claim to *Easy A is written by Bert V. Royal*. SemBERT passes this test and outputs SUPPORTS. Following the tests for semantic structure in Ribeiro et al. (2020)'s CheckList, we modify the evidence by changing the order of the propositions, creating symmetric relations and swapping them to active form. The new versions of the evidence are:

1. **Order change**: Easy A, stylized as easy A, is a 2010 American teen comedy film *written by Bert V. Royal, directed by Will Gluck*, and starring Emma Stone, [...]. ← **Refutes**

2. **Order change**: Easy A, stylized as easy A, is a 2010 American teen comedy film written by Bert V. Royal, starring Emma Stone, [...], *and directed by Will Gluck.* ← **Refutes**

3. **Symmetric relation**: Easy A, stylized as easy A, is a 2010 American teen comedy film *directed by Will Gluck and Bert V. Royal* and starring Emma Stone, [...]. ← **Supports**

4. **Remove the *written by* proposition**: Easy A, stylized as easy A, is a 2010 American teen comedy film directed by Will Gluck, and starring Emma Stone, [..]. ← **Refutes**

5. **Active form**: Easy A, stylized as easy A, is a

2010 American teen comedy film. *Will Gluck directed the film , and Bert V. Royal wrote it.* ← **Refutes**

With all the variations of the evidence presented above, SemBERT always outputs the right label, while BERT just outputs the right label in the last piece of evidence, which contains the same information but in active form. These tests suggest that SemBERT does have capabilities regarding semantic structure that are missing in BERT. However, more systematic tests should be performed in this direction.

6 Conclusion and Future Work

In this work we have investigated if semantic information could help to improve the reasoning process when inferring the truth label of a claim given some pieces of evidence. To this goal, we have used two different semantic parsers and the architecture of the pre-trained model SemBERT (Zhang et al., 2020a). For our experiments, we have used the FEVER dataset (Thorne et al., 2018), which requires building a model that, given some pieces of evidence, can output if a claim is supported, refuted, or the evidence does not give enough information.

We have performed several experiments on top of the SemBERT architecture, such as training models with different kinds of semantic information, different sets of semantic tags, and with an additional attention mechanism to represent the semantic information. In terms of label accuracy, all our experiments have outperformed the baseline, which was a BERT model with no additional semantic information. Our best model uses Semantic Role Labels and a set of 10 different tags, with no additional attention mechanism. This model achieves a label accuracy of 75.37 on the development set and 72.18 on the test set, outperforming the baseline by 1.5 and 1.3 percentage points respectively. Future work could include testing the impact of these semantic structures in models such as RoBERTa (Liu et al., 2019) or XLNet (Yang et al., 2019).

To better understand the contribution of the semantic information, we have performed some explainability tests with our best model. These have shown that the SRL knowledge might be contributing to guiding the model in semantically complex sentences that include several propositions or passive forms.

To keep moving towards systems that can contribute to the work of fact-checkers, future research on claim verification should take two directions. On the one hand, there is a need to develop large datasets that are more similar to naturally-occurring claims. On the other hand, NLI models for claim verification should output more explanatory justifications to their conclusions, which would make these systems more trust-worthy.

In this work, we have not dealt with the task of evidence retrieval. In FEVER, this task is limited by the static Wikipedia database that comes with the dataset. However, in real-world scenarios defining the boundaries of what is trust-worthy information is a challenge that goes beyond research in NLP and reaches the fields of journalism, politics and even philosophy. The non-static nature of what is a true fact is an additional challenge to evidence retrieval.

Acknowledgements

This work has been partially funded by the projects DeepText (KK-2020-00088, SPRI, Basque Government) and DeepReading (RTI2018-096846-B-C21, MCIU/AEI/FEDER, UE). Rodrigo Agerri acknowledges the funding of the UPV/EHU Colab 19/19 project "Tools for the analysis of parliamentary discourses: polarization, subjectivity and affectivity in the post-truth era", the RYC-2017–23647 fellowship and from the ANTIDOTE - EU CHIST-ERA project (PCI2020-120717-2) of the Agencia Estatal de Investigación through the INT-Acciones de Programación Conjunta Internacional (MINECO) 2020 call.

References

Pepa Atanasova, Jakob Grue Simonsen, Christina Lioma, and Isabelle Augenstein. 2020. A Diagnostic Study of Explainability Techniques for Text Classification. In *Proceedings of the 2020 Conference on Empirical Methods in Natural Language Processing (EMNLP)*, pages 3256–3274.

Isabelle Augenstein, Christina Lioma, Dongsheng Wang, Lucas Chaves Lima, Casper Hansen, Christian Hansen, and Jakob Grue Simonsen. 2019. MultiFC: A Real-World Multi-Domain Dataset for Evidence-Based Fact Checking of Claims. In *Proceedings of the 2019 Conference on Empirical Methods in Natural Language Processing and the 9th International Joint Conference on Natural Language Processing (EMNLP-IJCNLP)*, pages 4685–4697.

Collin F. Baker, Charles J. Fillmore, and John B. Lowe. 1998. The Berkeley FrameNet Project. In *Proceedings of the 36th Annual Meeting of the Association for Computational Linguistics and 17th International Conference on Computational Linguistics - Volume 1*, ACL '98/COLING '98, pages 86–90, USA. Association for Computational Linguistics.

Claire Bonial, Susan Brown, W. Corvey, Martha Palmer, Volha Petukhova, and Harry Bunt. 2011. An Exploratory Comparison of Thematic Roles in VerbNet and LIRICS.

Samuel Bowman, Gabor Angeli, Christopher Potts, and Christopher D Manning. 2015. A large annotated corpus for learning natural language inference. In *Proceedings of the 2015 Conference on Empirical Methods in Natural Language Processing*, pages 632–642.

Danqi Chen, Adam Fisch, Jason Weston, and Antoine Bordes. 2017a. Reading Wikipedia to Answer Open-Domain Questions. In *Proceedings of the 55th Annual Meeting of the Association for Computational Linguistics (Volume 1: Long Papers)*, pages 1870–1879.

Qian Chen, Xiaodan Zhu, Zhen-Hua Ling, Si Wei, Hui Jiang, and Diana Inkpen. 2017b. Enhanced LSTM for Natural Language Inference. In *Proceedings of the 55th Annual Meeting of the Association for Computational Linguistics (Volume 1: Long Papers)*, pages 1657–1668.

Soheil Danesh, Tamara Sumner, and James H. Martin. 2015. SGRank: Combining Statistical and Graphical Methods to Improve the State of the Art in Unsupervised Keyphrase Extraction. In *Proceedings of the Fourth Joint Conference on Lexical and Computational Semantics*, pages 117–126, Denver, Colorado. Association for Computational Linguistics.

Jacob Devlin, Ming-Wei Chang, Kenton Lee, and Kristina Toutanova. 2019. BERT: Pre-training of Deep Bidirectional Transformers for Language Understanding. In *Proceedings of the 2019 Conference of the North American Chapter of the Association for Computational Linguistics: Human Language Technologies, Volume 1 (Long and Short Papers)*, pages 4171–4186.

Javid Ebrahimi, Anyi Rao, Daniel Lowd, and Dejing Dou. 2018. HotFlip: White-Box Adversarial Examples for Text Classification. In *Proceedings of the 56th Annual Meeting of the Association for Computational Linguistics (Volume 2: Short Papers)*, pages 31–36.

Oren Etzioni, Michele Banko, Stephen Soderland, and Daniel Weld. 2008. Open Information Extraction from the Web. *Commun. ACM*, 51:68–74.

Matt Gardner, Joel Grus, Mark Neumann, Oyvind Tafjord, Pradeep Dasigi, Nelson F Liu, Matthew Peters, Michael Schmitz, and Luke Zettlemoyer. 2018. AllenNLP: A Deep Semantic Natural Language Processing Platform. In *Proceedings of Workshop for NLP Open Source Software (NLP-OSS)*, pages 1–6.

Andreas Hanselowski, Hao Zhang, Zile Li, Daniil Sorokin, Benjamin Schiller, Claudia Schulz, and Iryna Gurevych. 2018. UKP-Athene: Multi-Sentence Textual Entailment for Claim Verification. *EMNLP 2018*, page 103.

Luheng He, Mike Lewis, and Luke Zettlemoyer. 2015. Question-Answer Driven Semantic Role Labeling: Using Natural Language to Annotate Natural Language. In *Proceedings of the 2015 Conference on Empirical Methods in Natural Language Processing*, pages 643–653, Lisbon, Portugal. Association for Computational Linguistics.

Alfred Hermida. 2010. Twittering the news. *Journalism Practice*, 4:297–308.

Yichen Jiang, Shikha Bordia, Zheng Zhong, Charles Dognin, Maneesh Singh, and Mohit Bansal. 2020. HoVer: A Dataset for Many-Hop Fact Extraction And Claim Verification. In *Findings of the Association for Computational Linguistics: EMNLP 2020*, pages 3441–3460, Online. Association for Computational Linguistics.

Pieter-Jan Kindermans, Kristof Schütt, Klaus-Robert Müller, and Sven Dähne. 2016. Investigating the influence of noise and distractors on the interpretation of neural networks. *arXiv e-prints*, 1611:arXiv:1611.07270.

Karin Kipper, Hoa Trang Dang, and Martha Palmer. 2000. Class-Based Construction of a Verb Lexicon. In *Proceedings of the Seventeenth National Conference on Artificial Intelligence and Twelfth Conference on Innovative Applications of Artificial Intelligence*, pages 691–696. AAAI Press.

Amrith Krishna, Sebastian Riedel, and Andreas Vlachos. 2021. Proofver: Natural logic theorem proving for fact verification.

Nir Kshetri and Jeffrey Voas. 2017. The Economics of "Fake News". *IT Professional*, 19:8–12.

Mike Lewis, Yinhan Liu, Naman Goyal, Marjan Ghazvininejad, Abdelrahman Mohamed, Omer Levy, Veselin Stoyanov, and Luke Zettlemoyer. 2020. Bart: Denoising sequence-to-sequence pre-training for natural language generation, translation, and comprehension. *ACL*, abs/1910.13461.

Yinhan Liu, Myle Ott, Naman Goyal, Jingfei Du, Mandar Joshi, Danqi Chen, Omer Levy, Mike Lewis, Luke Zettlemoyer, and Veselin Stoyanov. 2019. RoBERTa: A Robustly Optimized BERT Pretraining Approach. *arXiv:1907.11692 [cs]*. ArXiv: 1907.11692.

Ilya Loshchilov and Frank Hutter. 2019. Decoupled Weight Decay Regularization. In *International Conference on Learning Representations*.

Mausam, Michael Schmitz, Stephen Soderland, Robert Bart, and Oren Etzioni. 2012. Open Language Learning for Information Extraction. In *Proceedings of the 2012 Joint Conference on Empirical Methods in Natural Language Processing and Computational Natural Language Learning*, pages 523–534, Jeju Island, Korea. Association for Computational Linguistics.

Yixin Nie, Haonan Chen, and Mohit Bansal. 2019. Combining fact extraction and verification with neural semantic matching networks. In *Proceedings of the AAAI Conference on Artificial Intelligence*, volume 33, pages 6859–6866. Issue: 01.

Rodrigo Nogueira and Kyunghyun Cho. 2020. Passage Re-ranking with BERT. *arXiv:1901.04085 [cs]*. ArXiv: 1901.04085.

Ray Oshikawa, Jing Qian, and William Yang Wang. 2020. A Survey on Natural Language Processing for Fake News Detection. In *Proceedings of the 12th Language Resources and Evaluation Conference*, pages 6086–6093, Marseille, France. European Language Resources Association.

Martha Palmer, Daniel Gildea, and Paul Kingsbury. 2005. The Proposition Bank: An Annotated Corpus of Semantic Roles. *Computational Linguistics*, 31(1):71–106.

Ankur Parikh, Oscar Täckström, Dipanjan Das, and Jakob Uszkoreit. 2016. A Decomposable Attention Model for Natural Language Inference. In *Proceedings of the 2016 Conference on Empirical Methods in Natural Language Processing*, pages 2249–2255, Austin, Texas. Association for Computational Linguistics.

Marco Tulio Ribeiro, Sameer Singh, and Carlos Guestrin. 2018. Semantically Equivalent Adversarial Rules for Debugging NLP models. In *Proceedings of the 56th Annual Meeting of the Association for Computational Linguistics (Volume 1: Long Papers)*, pages 856–865, Melbourne, Australia. Association for Computational Linguistics.

Marco Tulio Ribeiro, Tongshuang Wu, Carlos Guestrin, and Sameer Singh. 2020. Beyond Accuracy: Behavioral Testing of NLP Models with CheckList. In *Proceedings of the 58th Annual Meeting of the Association for Computational Linguistics*, pages 4902–4912, Online. Association for Computational Linguistics.

Peng Shi and Jimmy Lin. 2019. Simple BERT Models for Relation Extraction and Semantic Role Labeling. *arXiv:1904.05255 [cs]*. ArXiv: 1904.05255.

Karen Simonyan, Andrea Vedaldi, and Andrew Zisserman. 2014. Deep inside convolutional networks: Visualising image classification models and saliency maps. In *In Workshop at International Conference on Learning Representations*. Citeseer.

Amir Soleimani, Christof Monz, and Marcel Worring. 2019. *BERT for Evidence Retrieval and Claim Verification*. GroundAI.

J Springenberg, Alexey Dosovitskiy, Thomas Brox, and M Riedmiller. 2015. Striving for Simplicity: The All Convolutional Net. In *ICLR (workshop track)*.

Gabriel Stanovsky, Ido Dagan, and Mausam. 2015. Open IE as an Intermediate Structure for Semantic Tasks. In *Proceedings of the 53rd Annual Meeting of the Association for Computational Linguistics and the 7th International Joint Conference on Natural Language Processing (Volume 2: Short Papers)*, pages 303–308, Beijing, China. Association for Computational Linguistics.

Gabriel Stanovsky, Julian Michael, Luke Zettlemoyer, and Ido Dagan. 2018. Supervised Open Information Extraction. In *Proceedings of the 2018 Conference of the North American Chapter of the Association for Computational Linguistics: Human Language Technologies, Volume 1 (Long Papers)*, pages 885–895, New Orleans, Louisiana. Association for Computational Linguistics.

James Thorne and Andreas Vlachos. 2019. Adversarial attacks against Fact Extraction and VERification. *arXiv:1903.05543 [cs]*. ArXiv: 1903.05543.

James Thorne, Andreas Vlachos, Christos Christodoulopoulos, and Arpit Mittal. 2018. FEVER: a Large-scale Dataset for Fact Extraction and VERification. In *Proceedings of the 2018 Conference of the North American Chapter of the Association for Computational Linguistics: Human Language Technologies, Volume 1 (Long Papers)*, pages 809–819, New Orleans, Louisiana. Association for Computational Linguistics.

Soroush Vosoughi, Deb Roy, and Sinan Aral. 2018. The spread of true and false news online. *Science (New York, N.Y.)*, 359(6380):1146–1151.

David Wadden, Shanchuan Lin, Kyle Lo, Lucy Lu Wang, Madeleine van Zuylen, Arman Cohan, and Hannaneh Hajishirzi. 2020. Fact or Fiction: Verifying Scientific Claims. In *Proceedings of the 2020 Conference on Empirical Methods in Natural Language Processing (EMNLP)*, pages 7534–7550, Online. Association for Computational Linguistics.

Shuohang Wang and Jing Jiang. 2016. Learning Natural Language Inference with LSTM. *arXiv:1512.08849 [cs]*. ArXiv: 1512.08849.

William Yang Wang. 2017. "Liar, Liar Pants on Fire": A New Benchmark Dataset for Fake News Detection. In *Proceedings of the 55th Annual Meeting of the Association for Computational Linguistics (Volume 2: Short Papers)*, pages 422–426.

Adina Williams, Nikita Nangia, and Samuel Bowman. 2018. A Broad-Coverage Challenge Corpus for Sentence Understanding through Inference. In *Proceedings of the 2018 Conference of the North American Chapter of the Association for Computational Linguistics: Human Language Technologies, Volume 1 (Long Papers)*, pages 1112–1122, New Orleans,

Louisiana. Association for Computational Linguistics.

Zhilin Yang, Zihang Dai, Yiming Yang, Jaime Carbonell, Russ R Salakhutdinov, and Quoc V Le. 2019. Xlnet: Generalized autoregressive pretraining for language understanding. *Advances in neural information processing systems*, 32.

Fabio Massimo Zanzotto, Andrea Santilli, Leonardo Ranaldi, Dario Onorati, Pierfrancesco Tommasino, and Francesca Fallucchi. 2020. KERMIT: Complementing Transformer Architectures with Encoders of Explicit Syntactic Interpretations. In *Proceedings of the 2020 Conference on Empirical Methods in Natural Language Processing (EMNLP)*, pages 256–267, Online. Association for Computational Linguistics.

Matthew D Zeiler and Rob Fergus. 2014. Visualizing and understanding convolutional networks. In *European conference on computer vision*, pages 818–833. Springer.

Zhuosheng Zhang, Yuwei Wu, Hai Zhao, Zuchao Li, Shuailiang Zhang, Xi Zhou, and Xiang Zhou. 2020a. Semantics-Aware BERT for Language Understanding. *Proceedings of the AAAI Conference on Artificial Intelligence*, 34(05):9628–9635. Number: 05.

Zhuosheng Zhang, Yuwei Wu, Junru Zhou, Sufeng Duan, Hai Zhao, and Rui Wang. 2020b. SG-Net: Syntax-guided machine reading comprehension. In *Proceedings of the AAAI Conference on Artificial Intelligence*, volume 34, pages 9636–9643. Issue: 05.

Wanjun Zhong, Jingjing Xu, Duyu Tang, Zenan Xu, Nan Duan, Ming Zhou, Jiahai Wang, and Jian Yin. 2020. Reasoning Over Semantic-Level Graph for Fact Checking. In *Proceedings of the 58th Annual Meeting of the Association for Computational Linguistics*, pages 6170–6180, Online. Association for Computational Linguistics.

Jie Zhou, Xu Han, Cheng Yang, Zhiyuan Liu, Lifeng Wang, Changcheng Li, and Maosong Sun. 2019. GEAR: Graph-based Evidence Aggregating and Reasoning for Fact Verification. In *Proceedings of the 57th Annual Meeting of the Association for Computational Linguistics*, pages 892–901, Florence, Italy. Association for Computational Linguistics.

Xinyi Zhou and Reza Zafarani. 2020. A Survey of Fake News: Fundamental Theories, Detection Methods, and Opportunities. *ACM Computing Surveys*, 53(5):109:1–109:40.

Arkaitz Zubiaga, Ahmet Aker, Kalina Bontcheva, Maria Liakata, and Rob Procter. 2018. Detection and resolution of rumours in social media: A survey. *ACM Computing Surveys (CSUR)*, 51(2):1–36. Publisher: ACM New York, NY, USA.

A Appendix: Tags mapping

All Tags	Tags1 Tags	DREAM Tags
O	O	O
B-V	V	verb
I-V	V	verb
B-ARG0	ARG0	argument
I-ARG0	ARG0	argument
B-ARG1	ARG1	argument
I-ARG1	ARG1	argument
B-ARG2	ARG2	argument
I-ARG2	ARG2	argument
B-ARG4	ARG4	argument
I-ARG4	ARG4	argument
B-ARGM-TMP	TMP	temporal
I-ARGM-TMP	TMP	temporal
B-ARGM-LOC	LOC	location
I-ARGM-LOC	LOC	location
B-ARGM-CAU	ARGM	argument
I-ARGM-CAU	ARGM	argument
B-ARGM-PRP	ARGM	argument
I-ARGM-PRP	ARGM	argument

Table 4: Mapping between sets of SRL tags

PHEMEPlus: Enriching Social Media Rumour Verification with External Evidence

[1]John Dougrez-Lewis, [2,3]Elena Kochkina, [1,3]Miguel Arana-Catania, [1,2,3]Maria Liakata, [1,3]Yulan He
[1]Department of Computer Science, University of Warwick, UK
[2]Queen-Mary University of London, UK
[3]The Alan Turing Institute, UK
{j.Dougrez-Lewis,miguel.arana-catania,yulan.he}@warwick.ac.uk
{m.liakata,e.kochkina}@qmul.ac.uk

Abstract

Work on social media rumour verification utilises signals from posts, their propagation and users involved. Other lines of work target identifying and fact-checking claims based on information from Wikipedia, or trustworthy news articles without considering social media context. However works combining the information from social media with external evidence from the wider web are lacking. To facilitate research in this direction, we release a novel dataset, PHEMEPlus[1], an extension of the PHEME benchmark, which contains social media conversations as well as relevant external evidence for each rumour. We demonstrate the effectiveness of incorporating such evidence in improving rumour verification models. Additionally, as part of the evidence collection, we evaluate various ways of query formulation to identify the most effective method.

1 Introduction

The harm and prevalence of online misinformation made research into automated methods of information verification an important and active research area. This includes various tasks like fact-checking, social media rumour detection, stance classification and verification. In this work we are concerned with social media rumour verification, the task of identifying whether a rumour (i.e check-worthy claim circulating on social media whose veracity status is yet to be verified (Zubiaga et al., 2018)), is *True*, *False* or *Unverified*.

Although a significant amount of work has been done towards evaluating the veracity of social media rumours (Zubiaga et al., 2016; Ma et al., 2017; Song et al., 2018; Dougrez-Lewis et al., 2021), there is still a dearth of works and datasets combining the information from social media with external evidence from the wider web. While recent works focusing on rumours around the COVID-19 pandemic have been collecting data from a wide range of sources from news and social media to scientific publications (Cui and Lee, 2020; Zhou et al., 2020; Wang et al., 2020), these are not sufficient for the creation of generalisable verification models as they only focus on a single topic. At the same time works on fact-checking, which do not focus on social media content, but use claims from debunking websites (Lim et al., 2019; Ahmadi et al., 2019), as well as recent work by Li et al. (2021) have shown the benefits of utilising stance of evidence for verification.

Here we aim to further enable research in this direction and release an enriched version of a popular benchmark dataset PHEME (Zubiaga et al., 2016) with timely evidence for each of the rumours, obtained from a wide range of web sources.

Although a few works use web search for evidence retrieval (Popat et al., 2018; Lim et al., 2019), to our knowledge, only the work of Lim et al. (2017) touches upon the topic of the search query formulation. Here we analyse several query formulation strategies to find the most effective one.

In this work we make the following contributions:

- We collect and release the PHEMEPlus dataset of Twitter rumour conversations with the relevant heterogeneous evidence retrieved from the web to facilitate research on combining multiple sources of information for social media rumour verification.
- We investigate approaches towards search query formulation for evidence retrieval, together with evaluation metrics for the quality of evidence retrieved.
- We demonstrate the effectiveness of incorporating external evidence into rumour veracity classification models.

[1]https://github.com/JohnNLP/PhemePlus

Proceedings of the Fifth Fact Extraction and VERification Workshop (FEVER), pages 49 - 58
May 26, 2022 ©2022 Association for Computational Linguistics

2 Related work

2.1 Existing Veracity Classification Datasets

Among existing datasets for veracity classification we can broadly discern two categories: (1) focusing on claims arising from social media in the form of posts (Zubiaga et al., 2016; Ma et al., 2017) and (2) focusing on manually formulated claims, either created specifically for a task (Thorne et al., 2018), or consisting of titles from news or debunking websites (Wang, 2017; Alhindi et al., 2018; Lim et al., 2019; Ahmadi et al., 2019). These different types of claims present different challenges for verification models and evidence retrieval systems. In particular social media posts often use non-standard grammar, hashtags and have typos (intentional or otherwise). It can be crucial to process claims directly from social media to enable early-stage misinformation detection as rumours often start spreading on social media, later making it into the mainstream media. Only a few datasets incorporate both social media and evidence from the web, however these often focus on a very limited number of sources of evidence or a single topic (Dai et al., 2020; Cui and Lee, 2020). One of such datasets is FakeNewsNet (Shu et al., 2018) incorporating *fake* and *true* news articles from fact-checking websites PolitiFact[2] and GossipCop[3]. Articles are further augmented with users' posts on Twitter pertaining to them but not including full conversation structure. FakeHealth (Dai et al., 2020) is a similarly constructed dataset based on health-related news articles labelled by the Health News Review[4], including Twitter users' replies and profiles. Barrón-Cedeno et al. (2020) organised shared tasks for automatic identification and verification of claims in social media. Apart from tasks on check-worthiness estimation for tweets and verified claim retrieval, they also released tasks for supporting evidence retrieval and claim verification. However, the tasks mainly focused on misinformation about COVID-19 and the latter tasks were only offered in Arabic.

In light of the wave of misinformation associated with COVID-19 pandemic researchers have been collecting relevant datasets of scientific publications, news articles and their headlines, social media posts and claims about COVID-19 (Shaar et al., 2020; Dharawat et al., 2020; Zhou et al., 2020; Li et al., 2020; Memon and Carley, 2020; Hossain et al., 2020; Barrón-Cedeno et al., 2020). One of the most relevant work to ours is COAID (Cui and Lee, 2020), a large-scale dataset containing COVID-19 related news articles as well as social media posts. While these are rich resources, which enable further research against misinformation, they are insufficient for training generalisable models as they solely focus on one topic.

In this work we have augmented the PHEME dataset, a popular benchmark dataset for social media rumour verification, it contains rumours expressed via Twitter posts with full conversation threads from several news-breaking events on different topics. This dataset is set up to imitate realistic scenarios as (1) it was collected as the events were unfolding and then rumour stories were identified and annotated by a professional journalist as opposed to collecting tweets based on existing fact-checks as in Ma et al. (2017); and (2) the evaluation is performed in on events unseen during training. We augment it with evidence articles from across the web to give it access to an unlimited set of resources. To preserve the realistic scenario of verifying emerging rumours, all of our evidence is restricted to articles indexed by Google no later than the day on which the rumour was posted to Twitter.

2.2 Social Media Rumour Verification Models Using External Information

Social media rumour verification models use various types of information available on social media platform: text of rumourous posts and responses (Dougrez-Lewis et al., 2021), user information and connections (Khoo et al., 2020), propagation patterns (Ma et al., 2018). However, still only few works incorporate external evidence.

Lim et al. (2017) proposed the iFACT framework that extracts claims from tweets pertaining to major events. For each claim, it collects evidence from web search and estimates the likelihood of a claim being credible. To formulate the search query iFACT uses ClausIE (Del Corro and Gemulla, 2013) to extract (*subject, predicate, object*) triples from tweets. To determine the credibility of the claim iFACT uses features extracted from search results and dependencies between claims. Here we also experiment with using ClausIE to formulate the search query.

[2]https://www.politifact.com/

[3]https://www.suggest.com/

[4]https://www.healthnewsreview.org/

Events	Threads	True	False	Unverified	Relevant Articles
Charlie Hebdo	458	193	116	149	3941
Sydney Siege	522	382	86	54	4436
Ferguson	284	10	8	266	2473
Ottawa Shooting	470	329	72	69	4020
Germanwings Crash	238	94	111	33	2057
Total Threads	1972	1008	393	571	16927

Table 1: Statistics of the PHEMEPlus dataset by extending the PHEME-5 dataset with retrieved relevant articles. All but 2 rumours have at least 1 associated article.

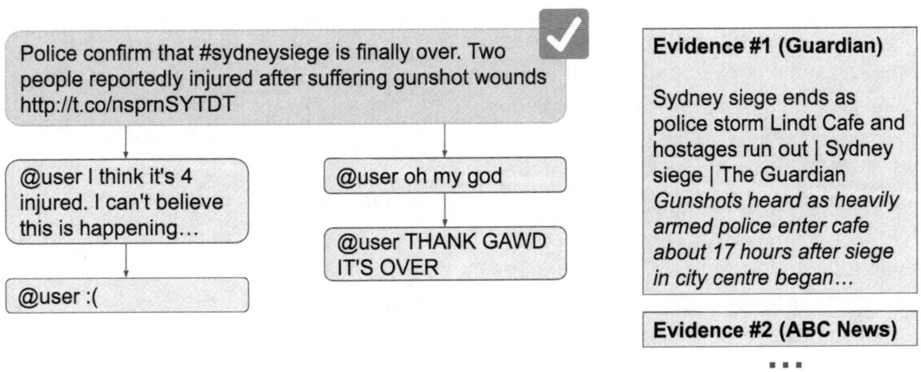

Figure 1: The PHEMEPlus dataset consists of labelled Twitter rumours, their conversation thread, and corresponding evidence retrieved from the web. This is an adapted example.

Li et al. (2021) propose to improve rumour detection on PHEME dataset by using evidence from Wikipedia. They first train the evidence extraction module on the FEVER dataset and then use it as part of a rumour detection system to get relevant sentences from a Wikipedia dump along with Twitter conversation around a rumour. While being limited by a single source of information, they demonstrate performance improvements over previous models not using external information.

In this work we use BERT-based models as strong baselines to demonstrate the effectiveness of incorporating the evidence for social media rumour verification. In future work we will be experimenting with various ways of incorporating it to maximise the benefits.

3 Augmenting PHEME dataset with External Evidence

3.1 Base dataset

We chose to extend the PHEME-5 dataset (Zubiaga et al., 2016), which consists of Twitter conversations discussing rumours around five real-world events including the Lindt Cafe siege in Sydney and the 2015 Charlie Hebdo terrorist attack. This dataset is a popular benchmark for rumour verification, it is particularly challenging due to class imbalance and evaluation using leave-one-event-out cross-validation, reflecting a real-world evaluation scenario. Table 1 shows the statistics of the PHEMEPlus dataset by extending the original PHEME-5 dataset with retrieved relevant articles. The first four columns show the number of conversation threads in each of the event and each of the classes in the orignal PHEME-5 dataset. Figure 1 shows an example entry in the PHEMEPlus dataset, comprised of a rumorous tweet, veracity label, its conversation thread, and relevant evidence retrieved from the web. It is notable that tweets in the conversation thread (and the rumour itself) often contain URLs provided by users which may be useful as a further source of evidence, and that the corresponding evidence is not a part of the original PHEME dataset. Kochkina (2019) has shown that *True* rumours in PHEME have a higher percentage of URLs attached (55%) than for *False* (48%)

and *Unverified* (48%) rumours. For the portion of PHEME with comments annotated for stance, these supplementary URLs were overwhelmingly found in comments *supporting* the source tweet's claim (33%) as opposed to those, *denying* (8%), *querying* (6%), or *commenting* (9%) on it.

3.2 Evidence Retrieval through Web search

In order to obtain evidence from the unlimited number of sources we chose to use Web search for evidence retrieval. We choose Google Search as it is one of the most established search engines, and, importantly, allows us to filter results by date. This is crucial as rumours are often resolved and widely debunked in some time following their originating event and the rumourous post, but this information would not be available to the model in a real time evaluation scenario.

Furthermore, the evidence we retrieve from Google appears robustly reputable, with popular news sources consistently ranking highly in the search results. This is to be expected, since their PageRank system weights heavily websites which are highly cited/referenced by others. Web search results are also more likely to be up-to-date than any corresponding Wikipedia pages regarding a current real world happening, which may not be updated nor appropriately checked for correctness.

For every search we include the term (before: date) at the start of the query to restrict results to articles from before the date the rumourous tweet was posted. For each query we collect the top 5 non-empty results from the web search.

While Google search is able to process various types of queries, from keywords to natural language utterances, we performed a set of experiments to identify the most suitable method of query formulation for our particular task of evidence retrieval for rumours conveyed in Twitter posts. We experiment with queries formulated as (1) natural language sentence, (2) keywords, and (3) *(subject, object, predicate)* triples. For each experiment, we include around 99% of the PHEME dataset since a few queries did not yield enough non-empty results. Although we are aware of some more advanced studies into query expansion and formulation (Tamannaee et al., 2020; Scells et al., 2020), contributing to these fields is beyond the scope of this paper. Here we aim to demonstrate gains from relatively simple approaches described below towards evidence retrieval.

3.2.1 Search Strategies

We experiment with the following search strategies:

Preprocessed The search query is the source rumour, obtained from the preprocessed tweet. Our preprocessing entails removing URLs, replacing user mentions with "user" (so as to retain lexical structure), removing hashtags from the end but not the middle (also for lexical structure) and segmenting any compound hashtags. URLs are saved aside since they may have future use as evidence. Hashtags at the end of the tweet (but not others) are also retained, placed in brackets for an "OR" search with the rest of the query. These hashtags in particular are expected to be highly telling of the topic/theme of the tweet, especially when it is otherwise lacking in contextual words.

Shortening with StanfordNLP We use Stanza (Qi et al., 2020) to parse preprocessed tweets. Having obtained a parse tree, words in the following constructs are retained in-place: {*obl:npmod, compound, advcl, nummod, acl:relcl, nsubj:pass, acl, amod, aux:pass*}. This combination of constructs was iteratively finetuned until the resultant queries felt similar to the author's own search style, the idea being to replicate the search strategy of an experienced user. Hashtags at the end of tweets are handled as before.

Shortening with ClausIE We use ClausIE (Del Corro and Gemulla, 2013), a popular subject-relation-object extraction system in the same manner to find (*subject, predicate, object*) triples. These are kept in-place whilst the other words are removed. Hashtags at the end of tweets are retained as before.

Examples of the search queries formed can be found in Table 2.

3.2.2 Evaluation metrics

We devise evaluation metrics to compare the quality of evidence retrieved using different query types, without the need for a rumour verification model in advance.

URL Words Metric URLs frequently contain English words which are representative of the content on their webpage, which we can treat as gold-standard keywords as in (Ma et al., 2016). To get a goodness score in the range [0,1] we compute the cosine similarity between the words in URLs of retrieved articles and those posted in re-

Original Rumour:	*MORE: Massacre suspects believed to have taken hostage and holed up in small industrial town northeast of Paris: <url> #CharlieHebdo*
Query Strategy	**Query Text**
Preprocessed	before:2015-01-09 MORE : Massacre suspects believed to have taken hostage and holed up in small industrial town northeast of Paris :
StanfordNLP	before:2015-01-09 (Charlie Hebdo) Massacre suspects small industrial town northeast
ClausIE	before:2015-01-09 (Charlie Hebdo) Massacre suspects believed to have taken hostage holed up in small industrial town northeast of Paris

Table 2: Examples of search queries generated by the various search strategies, given the original rumour. In this case, the ClausIE strategy only removes the words "MORE" and "and".

sponse to the rumour. Specifically, for each retrieved article, its URL-words are compared with those of each URL in the Twitter comments. The final score is the average of all such cosine similarities across all retrieved articles in the dataset, encoded by Word2Vec (Mikolov et al., 2013).

GloVe Metric If an article is relevant to a rumour, they will be similar in content. We use GloVe (Pennington et al., 2014) to calculate the similarity between the first 3 paragraphs of an article and the source rumour, with the title also counting as a paragraph. We use only the first few paragraphs because they seem likely to contain the highest density of relevant information. Cosine similarity scores are calculated between each of these paragraphs and the source rumour, and are averaged to give the article a similarity score. Unknown words with zero vectors are ignored for this purpose, although there is a weakness that some of the most important event-specific words could be unknown.

BERTScore Metric This is calculated similarly to the GloVe metric, except that BERTScore (Zhang et al., 2020) is used in its place.

3.2.3 Evaluating Retrieval Results

Table 3 displays the performance of our search strategies when evaluated via the URL Words, GloVe, and BERT evaluation metrics. These results suggest that searching for the preprocessed tweet may be the best way to get relevant background information from the web, as opposed to extracting keywords from the tweet. This narrowly surpasses the performance of our ClausIE-based search strategy, which outperforms the StanfordNLP approach. The ClausIE strategy may retain a higher proportion of key grammatical constructs than the latter, which play an unexpectedly important role in Google's search algorithm. This is contrary to the authors' searching intuition, perhaps due to their recent integration of models such as BERT (Devlin et al., 2018).

Metric	Preprocessed	StanfordNLP	ClausIE
URL Words	**0.802**	0.777	0.795
GloVe	**0.661**	0.651	0.660
BERTScore	**0.826**	0.825	0.825

Table 3: Performance of the search strategies, evaluated by our evaluation metrics.

Although some of the values in Table 3 appear close together, it is notable that the results of the different query formulations land in the same order irrespective of the scoring metric used. Furthermore, the score differences between different query formulations become more substantial when taking into account their weak upper and lower bounds derived from using artificially generated 'target article' and 'random' queries (data not shown).

3.3 PHEMEPlus dataset

An example entry of the PHEMEPlus dataset can be found in Figure 1. The number of articles we retrieved using the *Preprocessed* method can be found in Table 1. All but two of the rumours have at least one associated evidence article, up to a maximum of 10.

We explore the overlap between the evidence in our resultant PHEMEPlus dataset and the URLs in the Twitter comments responding to the rumours. Table 4 shows the overlap between the articles retrieved from web search (using the Preprocessed Only strategy) and those from the Twitter comments. We observe little overlap between articles retrieved from web search and articles retrieved

	Overall pages	Unique pages
From web search	13255 (12008 not-empty)	3817 (3425 not-empty)
From rumour responses	2160 (1658 not-empty)	601 (457 not-empty)
Overlap	100	102

Table 4: Overlap of retrieved articles with articles from rumour responses.

from comments responding to rumours. The latter may thus be a substantially different, potentially less useful, source of evidence due to a high density of social media pages and the likelihood that some of the comments may not be directly responding to the source rumour.

A relatively large proportion of the articles retrieved from responses are deemed "empty", meaning they either have no body-text and/or no title. From this, and manual inspection, we infer that response-URLs are more likely to be social media posts or videos which are prone to missing titles or first paragraphs.

The overall:unique ratio being similar for both thread and web suggests that the Google results are indeed sensitive to the content of each thread, as opposed to repeatedly giving the same results for a given rumourous event. There is not much overlap between the search results and the Twitter thread, and a large proportion of existing overlap might be explainable by news websites tweeting their news URLs. This is not attributable to overly stringent overlap criteria as the discrepancy between the overall number of articles and the number of articles without duplicates acts as a positive control to this end.

Similar links nearly always result from the same thread, possibly due to the aforementioned news companies. Investigating further, the vast majority (if not all) of the overlap was news articles. Speculatively, it is plausible that most of this overlap came from news websites tweeting their stories, as there are some examples of this in the dataset.

4 Evaluating the Effectiveness of Evidence for Rumour Verification

We conduct experiments to evaluate the effectiveness of our retrieved evidence for Twitter rumour veracity classification.

4.1 Evidence Sentence Retrieval

In our PHEMEPlus dataset, each source tweet is paired with up to 10 most relevant retrieved articles. We follow the typical pipeline fact checking approach to further select the 5 most relevant sentences from the articles associated with each source tweet. In order to do this, we use a simple novel approach based on ClausIE (Del Corro and Gemulla, 2013). The idea is to be able to reliably find relevant sentences whilst not being clobbered by the inevitably rare rumour-specific vocabulary which may not be recognised by many approaches. First, we use ClausIE to extract all relevant subject-predicate-object triples from the retrieved information. We assume these to be the words with the most potential for true relevance to the tweet. Any stop-words contained within are filtered out. For each sentence, a score is assigned based on how many of these important words are also contained in the tweet, penalising both overly long (>20 token) and short (<5 token) sentences as are likely to be either uninformative or unconcise and work poorly with the BERT models. In particular, short sentences are ignored, whereas long sentences lose 2% of their score for each additional word. Only rumours with enough evidence to extract 5 sentences as above are used (99% of them) in our experiments. The top 5 such sentences are paired with each source tweet and are fed into a rumour classification model for veracity assessment.

4.2 Veracity Classification Models

We compare the performance of several veracity classification models in three input scenarios: (1) rumour (i.e., source tweet) alone, (2) evidence (i.e., extracted sentences) alone and (3) rumour concatenated with the evidence (extracted sentences). The classification models chosen include pre-trained language models such as BERT (Devlin et al., 2018) and RoBERTa (Liu et al., 2019), and a model making use of natural language inference results between a source rumour and its related evidence sentence.

BERT-based approaches We train BERT-based models including BERT and RoBERTa followed by a single softmax layer for rumour verification. Each pair of a rumour and a piece of relevant evidence sentence is concatenated as input to the model. The

BERT	Ch	Fe	Ge	Ot	Sy	False	True	Unv	MacroF1
Rumour + Ev.	**0.317**	**0.174**	0.213	**0.406**	0.318	**0.221**	0.549	**0.265**	**0.345**
Rumour	0.306	0.134	**0.315**	0.345	**0.320**	0.209	0.562	0.242	0.338
Evidence	0.268	0.045	0.264	0.370	0.307	0.140	**0.645**	0.099	0.295
RoBERTa									
Rumour + Ev.	**0.306**	**0.183**	**0.383**	0.368	**0.347**	**0.384**	0.600	**0.279**	**0.421**
Rumour	0.290	0.113	0.260	**0.420**	0.309	0.211	0.549	0.232	0.331
Evidence	0.288	0.028	0.252	0.335	0.327	0.145	**0.611**	0.144	0.301
NLI-SAN									
Rumour + Ev.	**0.354**	**0.256**	**0.365**	**0.591**	**0.458**	**0.186**	**0.480**	**0.250**	**0.405**

Table 5: Per-event and per-fold F1 scores from the BERT, RoBERTa, and NLI-SAN models. The 2-letter column headings abbreviate the names of individual rumourous events in PHEME (as in Table 1).

final predictions were determined by majority voting. These particular models are chosen because flavours of BERT have previously achieved state-of-the-art results in many natural language processing tasks.

Self-Attention Network based on Natural Language Inference (NLI-SAN) This method uses not only the representation of rumour and evidence like the previous methods, but also the Natural Language Inference (NLI) relationship between them.

First each rumour is paired with each of the evidence sentences and is fed into the RoBERTa-large-MNLI[5] model to generate the NLI relation triplet representing the *contradiction*, *neutrality*, and *entailment* probabilities. The rumour-sentence pair is also fed into the RoBERTa-large[5] model to generate the contextual representation. Both outputs are then combined using a self-attention network in which the NLI relation triplet is used as the query, while the contextual representation is used as the key and value. Afterwards, all the outputs are concatenated into a single output that is passed through a Multi-Layer Perceptron (MLP) and a Softmax layer that generates the final veracity classification value.

Since this approach relies on the inference relationship between rumour and evidence, we will only compare it with the other models if both elements are available, and thus only one result is shown in Table 5.

4.3 Experimental Setup

Experiments were performed using 5-fold leave-one-out-cross-validation with each of PHEME's rumourous events being a fold, as is customary for this dataset (see Section 3.1). We will release the code used to collect the evidence and to perform experiments on GitHub.

For the training of the aforementioned models, the inputs are padded and truncated to the longest sequence. Cross-entropy is used as the loss function. The optimizer used is AdamW (Loshchilov and Hutter, 2019) with $\beta_1 = 0.9$, $\beta_2 = 0.999$, and a weight decay of 0.01. For the BERT-based models, the batch size is 20, the learning rate is 3×10^{-5}, and the training is performed for 25 epochs. For NLI-SAN, the size of the hidden layer is 50, the batch size is 30, the learning rate is 10^{-4}, and the training is performed for 200 epochs.

4.4 Results and Discussion

Table 5 presents the results of our experiments in terms of macro-averaged F1-score. Macro F1 score is a suitable metric to evaluate performance on this dataset due to class and fold size imbalance.

In these experiments it is not our goal to outperform state-of-the-art results on the PHEME dataset, but to demonstrate the effectiveness of incorporating the evidence for social media rumour verification. State-of-the-art results are obtained by more complex architectures, in which incorporating the evidence and evaluating its effects is a more challenging task. For instance, the VRoC model (Cheng et al., 2020) currently yields state-of-the-art F1 score of 0.484 on this task, it uses Variational Autoencoder for representation of the rumour as well as multitask learning set up incorporating four tasks.

The results in Table 5 suggest that there is indeed a benefit to using the evidence which we have retrieved for rumour veracity classification. This joint approach outperforms the other two, and the

[5]`https://huggingface.co/`

use of the rumour alone generally outperforms the use of evidence alone, fitting with the idea that veracity can be classified to some extent by the writing style of the rumour alone.

In addition to the improvement in the results obtained by having evidence relevant to each rumour, our work opens the door to the use of more complex veracity classification models that consider additional attributes between both elements. The results obtained in the case of the NLI-SAN model show how this approach can be useful, obtaining better results than using the BERT model, although in this case inferior to the more simple use of RoBERTa.

A more detailed, per-class and per-fold, results breakdown for all of the models can be found in Table 5. For both BERT and RoBERTa, the combination of rumour together with evidence seems particularly useful for correct classification of the *False* class, with a mild gain also noted for *Unverified*. This could be the result of models inferring that there is disagreement between *False* rumours and their evidence, which would not be possible without the presence of both sources. It is noteworthy that existing rumour veracity classification models using the PHEME dataset have often found the False and Unverified classes to be problematic (Dougrez-Lewis et al., 2021). *True* class also benefits from incorporating evidence in RoBERTa model comparing to using rumour only. The results breakdown for the NLI-SAN model can also be found in Table 5, for which a similar pattern of per-class results can be observed. Most of the per-fold results for both BERT and RoBERTa also show the best performance when using a combination of rumour and evidence, only with exception of Germanwings Crash event (dominated by *False* class) for BERT and Ottawa shooting event (dominated by *True* class) for RoBERTa.

5 Conclusions and Future Work

After experimentation with various searching strategies for retrieving evidence from the web, we have constructed the PHEMEPlus dataset, which will facilitate further work on using evidence from wide range of sources for rumour veracity classification. The best such strategies, according to our evaluation metrics, are those which leave the grammatical structure of the claim relatively intact. There is much potential to improve existing rumour veracity classification systems by augmenting them with, or with a broader range, or better quality of evidence. We plan to build upon these findings in the future, working on identifying ways of incorporating the evidence from heterogeneous sources into more complex rumour verification models to maximise the gains from this information and achieve state-of-the-art results.

6 Acknowledgements

This work was supported by an EPSRC grant (EP/V048597/1). JDL was funded by the EPSRC Doctoral Training Grant. ML and YH are supported by Turing AI Fellowships (EP/V030302/1, EP/V020579/1).

References

Naser Ahmadi, Joohyung Lee, Paolo Papotti, and Mohammed Saeed. 2019. Explainable fact checking with probabilistic answer set programming.

Tariq Alhindi, Savvas Petridis, and Smaranda Muresan. 2018. Where is your evidence: improving fact-checking by justification modeling. In *Proceedings of the first workshop on fact extraction and verification (FEVER)*, pages 85–90.

Alberto Barrón-Cedeno, Tamer Elsayed, Preslav Nakov, Giovanni Da San Martino, Maram Hasanain, Reem Suwaileh, and Fatima Haouari. 2020. Checkthat! at clef 2020: Enabling the automatic identification and verification of claims in social media. In *European Conference on Information Retrieval*, pages 499–507. Springer.

Mingxi Cheng, Shahin Nazarian, and Paul Bogdan. 2020. *VRoC: Variational Autoencoder-Aided Multi-Task Rumor Classifier Based on Text*, page 2892–2898. Association for Computing Machinery, New York, NY, USA.

Limeng Cui and Dongwon Lee. 2020. Coaid: Covid-19 healthcare misinformation dataset. *arXiv preprint arXiv:2006.00885*.

Enyan Dai, Yiwei Sun, and Suhang Wang. 2020. Ginger cannot cure cancer: Battling fake health news with a comprehensive data repository. In *Proceedings of the International AAAI Conference on Web and Social Media*, volume 14, pages 853–862.

Luciano Del Corro and Rainer Gemulla. 2013. Clausie: Clause-based open information extraction. In *Proceedings of the 22nd International Conference on World Wide Web*, WWW '13, page 355–366, New York, NY, USA. Association for Computing Machinery.

Jacob Devlin, Ming-Wei Chang, Kenton Lee, and Kristina Toutanova. 2018. Bert: Pre-training of deep bidirectional transformers for language understanding.

Arkin Dharawat, Ismini Lourentzou, Alex Morales, and ChengXiang Zhai. 2020. Drink bleach or do what now? covid-hera: A dataset for risk-informed health decision making in the presence of covid19 misinformation. *arXiv preprint arXiv:2010.08743*.

John Dougrez-Lewis, Maria Liakata, Elena Kochkina, and Yulan He. 2021. Learning disentangled latent topics for twitter rumour veracity classification. In *Findings of the Association for Computational Linguistics: ACL-IJCNLP 2021*, pages 3902–3908.

Tamanna Hossain, Robert L Logan IV, Arjuna Ugarte, Yoshitomo Matsubara, Sean Young, and Sameer Singh. 2020. Covidlies: Detecting covid-19 misinformation on social media. In *Proceedings of the 1st Workshop on NLP for COVID-19 (Part 2) at EMNLP 2020*.

Ling Min Serena Khoo, Hai Leong Chieu, Zhong Qian, and Jing Jiang. 2020. Interpretable rumor detection in microblogs by attending to user interactions. In *Proceedings of the AAAI Conference on Artificial Intelligence*, volume 34, pages 8783–8790.

Elena Kochkina. 2019. Rumour stance and veracity classification in social media conversations,".

Jiawen Li, Shiwen Ni, and Hung-Yu Kao. 2021. Meet the truth: Leverage objective facts and subjective views for interpretable rumor detection. In *Findings of the Association for Computational Linguistics: ACL-IJCNLP 2021*, pages 705–715.

Yichuan Li, Bohan Jiang, Kai Shu, and Huan Liu. 2020. Mm-covid: A multilingual and multimodal data repository for combating covid-19 disinformation. *arXiv preprint arXiv:2011.04088*.

Wee Yong Lim, Mong Li Lee, and Wynne Hsu. 2017. Ifact: An interactive framework to assess claims from tweets. In *Proceedings of the 2017 ACM on Conference on Information and Knowledge Management*, CIKM '17, page 787–796, New York, NY, USA. Association for Computing Machinery.

Wee Yong Lim, Mong Li Lee, and Wynne Hsu. 2019. End-to-end time-sensitive fact check,". In *ACM SIGIR Workshop on Reducing Online Misinformation Exposure (ROME)*.

Yinhan Liu, Myle Ott, Naman Goyal, Jingfei Du, Mandar Joshi, Danqi Chen, Omer Levy, Mike Lewis, Luke Zettlemoyer, and Veselin Stoyanov. 2019. Roberta: A robustly optimized bert pretraining approach.

Ilya Loshchilov and Frank Hutter. 2019. Decoupled weight decay regularization. In *International Conference on Learning Representations*.

Jing Ma, Wei Gao, Prasenjit Mitra, Sejeong Kwon, Bernard J. Jansen, Kam-Fai Wong, and Meeyoung Cha. 2016. Detecting rumors from microblogs with recurrent neural networks. In *Proceedings of the Twenty-Fifth International Joint Conference on Artificial Intelligence*, IJCAI'16, page 3818–3824. AAAI Press.

Jing Ma, Wei Gao, and Kam-Fai Wong. 2017. Detect rumors in microblog posts using propagation structure via kernel learning. In *Proceedings of the 55th Annual Meeting of the Association for Computational Linguistics (Volume 1: Long Papers)*, pages 708–717, Vancouver, Canada. Association for Computational Linguistics.

Jing Ma, Wei Gao, and Kam-Fai Wong. 2018. Rumor detection on twitter with tree-structured recursive neural networks. In *Proceedings of the 56th Annual Meeting of the Association for Computational Linguistics (Volume 1: Long Papers)*, volume 1, pages 1980–1989.

Shahan Ali Memon and Kathleen M Carley. 2020. Characterizing covid-19 misinformation communities using a novel twitter dataset. In *CEUR Workshop Proceedings*, volume 2699.

Tomas Mikolov, Ilya Sutskever, Kai Chen, Greg Corrado, and Jeffrey Dean. 2013. Distributed representations of words and phrases and their compositionality. In *Proceedings of the 26th International Conference on Neural Information Processing Systems - Volume 2*, NIPS'13, page 3111–3119, Red Hook, NY, USA. Curran Associates Inc.

Jeffrey Pennington, Richard Socher, and Christopher Manning. 2014. GloVe: Global vectors for word representation. In *Proceedings of the 2014 Conference on Empirical Methods in Natural Language Processing (EMNLP)*, pages 1532–1543, Doha, Qatar. Association for Computational Linguistics.

Kashyap Popat, Subhabrata Mukherjee, Jannik Strötgen, and Gerhard Weikum. 2018. Credeye: A credibility lens for analyzing and explaining misinformation. In *Companion Proceedings of the The Web Conference 2018*, WWW '18, page 155–158, Republic and Canton of Geneva, CHE. International World Wide Web Conferences Steering Committee.

Peng Qi, Yuhao Zhang, Yuhui Zhang, Jason Bolton, and Christopher D. Manning. 2020. Stanza: A Python natural language processing toolkit for many human languages. In *Proceedings of the 58th Annual Meeting of the Association for Computational Linguistics: System Demonstrations*.

Harrisen Scells, Guido Zuccon, Bevan Koopman, and Justin Clark. 2020. Automatic boolean query formulation for systematic review literature search. In *Proceedings of The Web Conference 2020*, pages 1071–1081.

Shaden Shaar, Alex Nikolov, Nikolay Babulkov, Firoj Alam, Alberto Barrón-Cedeno, Tamer Elsayed, Maram Hasanain, Reem Suwaileh, Fatima Haouari, Giovanni Da San Martino, et al. 2020. Overview of checkthat! 2020 english: Automatic identification and verification of claims in social media. In *CLEF (Working Notes)*.

Kai Shu, Deepak Mahudeswaran, Suhang Wang, Dongwon Lee, and Huan Liu. 2018. Fakenewsnet: A data repository with news content, social context and spatialtemporal information for studying fake news on social media. *arXiv preprint arXiv:1809.01286*.

Changhe Song, Cunchao Tu, Cheng Yang, Zhiyuan Liu, and Maosong Sun. 2018. Ced: Credible early detection of social media rumors.

Mahtab Tamannaee, Hossein Fani, Fattane Zarrinkalam, Jamil Samouh, Samad Paydar, and Ebrahim Bagheri. 2020. Reque: A configurable workflow and dataset collection for query refinement. In *Proceedings of the 29th ACM International Conference on Information and Knowledge Management*, CIKM '20, page 3165–3172, New York, NY, USA. Association for Computing Machinery.

James Thorne, Andreas Vlachos, Christos Christodoulopoulos, and Arpit Mittal. 2018. FEVER: a large-scale dataset for fact extraction and VERification. In *Proceedings of the 2018 Conference of the North American Chapter of the Association for Computational Linguistics: Human Language Technologies, Volume 1 (Long Papers)*, pages 809–819, New Orleans, Louisiana. Association for Computational Linguistics.

Lucy Lu Wang, Kyle Lo, Yoganand Chandrasekhar, Russell Reas, Jiangjiang Yang, Doug Burdick, Darrin Eide, Kathryn Funk, Yannis Katsis, Rodney Michael Kinney, et al. 2020. Cord-19: The covid-19 open research dataset. In *Proceedings of the 1st Workshop on NLP for COVID-19 at ACL 2020*.

William Yang Wang. 2017. " liar, liar pants on fire": A new benchmark dataset for fake news detection. *arXiv preprint arXiv:1705.00648*.

Tianyi Zhang, Varsha Kishore, Felix Wu, Kilian Q. Weinberger, and Yoav Artzi. 2020. Bertscore: Evaluating text generation with bert.

Xinyi Zhou, Apurva Mulay, Emilio Ferrara, and Reza Zafarani. 2020. Recovery: A multimodal repository for covid-19 news credibility research. In *International Conference on Information and Knowledge Management, Proceedings*.

Arkaitz Zubiaga, Ahmet Aker, Kalina Bontcheva, Maria Liakata, and Rob Procter. 2018. Detection and resolution of rumours in social media: A survey. *ACM Comput. Surv.*, 51(2).

Arkaitz Zubiaga, Maria Liakata, Rob Procter, Geraldine Wong Sak Hoi, and Peter Tolmie. 2016. Analysing how people orient to and spread rumours in social media by looking at conversational threads. *PloS one*, 11(3):e0150989.

XInfoTabS: Evaluating Multilingual Tabular Natural Language Inference

Bhavnick Minhas[1*], **Anant Shankhdhar**[1*], **Vivek Gupta**[2*†], **Divyanshu Aggrawal**[3], **Shuo Zhang**[4]

[1]Indian Institute of Technology, Guwahati; [2]School of Computing, University of Utah

[3]Delhi Technological University; [4]Bloomberg

{bhavnick, anant.shankhdhar}@iitg.ac.in; vgupta@cs.utah.edu;

divyanshuggrwl@gmail.com; szhang611@bloomberg.net

Abstract

The ability to reason about tabular or semi-structured knowledge is a fundamental problem for today's Natural Language Processing (NLP) systems. While significant progress has been achieved in the direction of tabular reasoning, these advances are limited to English due to the absence of multilingual benchmark datasets for semi-structured data. In this paper, we use machine translation methods to construct a multilingual tabular natural language inference (TNLI) dataset, namely XInfoTabS, which expands the English TNLI dataset of InfoTabS to ten diverse languages. We also present several baselines for multilingual tabular reasoning, e.g., machine translation-based methods and cross-lingual TNLI. We discover that the XInfoTabS evaluation suite is both practical and challenging. As a result, this dataset will contribute to increased linguistic inclusion in tabular reasoning research and applications.

1 Introduction

Natural Language Inference (NLI) on semi-structured knowledge like tables is a crucial challenge for existing (NLP) models. Recently, two datasets, TabFact (Chen et al., 2019) on Wikipedia relational tables and InfoTabS (Gupta et al., 2020) on Wikipedia Infoboxes, have been proposed to investigate this problem. Among the solutions, contextual models such as BERT (Devlin et al., 2019) and RoBERTa (Liu et al., 2019), when adapted for tabular data, surprisingly achieve remarkable performance.

The recent development of multi-lingual extensions of contextualizing models such as mBERT (Devlin et al., 2019) from BERT and XLM-RoBERTa (Conneau et al., 2020) from RoBERTa, has led to substantial interest in the problem of multi-lingual NLI and the creation of multi-lingual XNLI (Conneau et al., 2018) and TaxiXNLI (K et al., 2021) dataset from English MNLI (Williams et al., 2018) dataset. However, there is still no equivalent multi-lingual NLI dataset for semi-structured tabular data. To fill this gap, we propose XInfoTabS, a multi-lingual extension of InfoTabS dataset. The XInfoTabS dataset consists of ten languages, namely English ('en'), German ('de'), French ('fr'), Spanish ('es'), Afrikaans ('af'), Russian ('ru'), Chinese ('zh'), Korean ('ko'), Hindi ('hi') and Arabic ('ar'), which belong to seven distinct language families and six unique writing scripts. Furthermore, these languages are the majority spoken in all seven continents covering 2.76 billion native speakers in comparison to 360 million English language (InfoTabS) speakers[1].

The intuitive method of constructing XInfoTabS, i.e., human-driven manual translation, is too expensive in terms of money and time. Alternatively, various state-of-the-art machine translation models, such as mBART50 (Tang et al., 2020), MarianMT (Junczys-Dowmunt et al., 2018), M2M100 (Fan et al., 2020a), have greatly enhanced translation quality across a broad variety of languages. Furthermore, NLI requires simply that the translation models retain the semantics of the premises and hypotheses, which machine translation can deliver (K et al., 2021). Therefore, we use automatic machine translation models to construct XInfoTabS from InfoTabS.

Tabular data is far more challenging to translate than semantically complete and grammatical sentences with existing state-of-the-art translation systems. To mitigate this challenge, we propose an efficient, high-quality translation pipeline that utilizes Name Entity Recognition (NER) and table context in the form of category information to convert table cells into structured sentences before

*Equal Contribution †Corresponding Author

[1] Refer to Appendix Table 5 for more information.

Proceedings of the Fifth Fact Extraction and VERification Workshop (FEVER), pages 59 - 77
May 26, 2022

Boxing (en)		Boxe (fr)	
Focus	Punching, striking	Focus	Punching, frappe
Olympic sport	688 BC (Ancient Greece), 1904 (modern)	Sport olympique	688 av. J.-C. (Grèce ancienne), 1904 (moderne)
Parenthood	Bare-knuckle boxing	Parentalité	Bare-knuckle boxe
Country of origin	Prehistoric	Pays d'origine	Préhistorique
Also known as	Western Boxing, Pugilism See note.	Aussi connu sous le nom	Western Boxing, Pugilism Voir note.

Language	Hypothesis	Label
English	The modern form of boxing started in the late 1900's.	CONTRADICTION
German	Boxen hat seinen Ursprung als olympischer Sport, der vor Jahrtausenden begann.	CONTRADICTION
French	La boxe occidentale implique des punches et des frappes	ENTAILMENT
Spanish	El boxeo ha sido un evento olímpico moderno durante más de 100 años.	ENTAILMENT
Afrikaans	Bare-knuckle boks is 'n prehistoriese vorm van boks.	NEUTRAL

Table 1: An example of the XInfoTabS dataset containing English (top-left) and French (top-right) tables in parallel with the hypothesis associated with the table in five languages (below).

translation. We assess the translations via several automatic and human verification methods to ensure quality. Our translations were found to be accurate for the majority of languages, with German and Arabic having the most and least exact translations, respectively. Table 1 shows an example from the XINFOTABS dataset.

We conduct tabular NLI experiments using XINFOTABS in monolingual and multilingual settings. By doing so, we aim to assess the capacity and cross-lingual transferability of state-of-the-art multilingual models such as mBERT (Devlin et al., 2019), and XLM-Roberta (Conneau et al., 2020). Our investigations reveal that these multilingual models, when assessed for additional languages, perform comparably to English. Second, the translation-based technique outperforms all other approaches on the adversarial evaluation sets for multilingual tabular NLI in terms of performance. Thirdly, the method of intermediate-task finetuning, also known as pre-finetuning, significantly improves performance by finetuning on additional languages prior to the target language. Finally, these models perform admirably on cross-lingual tabular NLI (tables and hypotheses given in different languages), although the additional effort is required to improve them. Our contributions are as follows:

- We introduce XINFOTABS, a multi-lingual extension of INFOTABS, a semi-structured tabular inference English dataset over ten diverse languages.
- We propose an efficient pipeline for high-quality translations of semi-structured tabular data using state-of-the-art translation models.
- We conduct intensive inference experiments on XINFOTABS and evaluate the performance of state-of-the-art multilingual models with various strategies.

The dataset and associated scripts, is available at `https://xinfotabs.github.io/`.

2 Why the INFOTABS dataset?

There are only two public datasets, both in English, available for semi-structured tabular reasoning, namely TabFact (Chen et al., 2019) and INFOTABS (Gupta et al., 2020). We choose INFOTABS because it includes multiple adversarial test sets for model evaluation. Additionally, the INFOTABS dataset also includes the NEUTRAL label, which is absent in TabFact. The INFOTABS dataset contains 2,540 tables serving as premise and 23,738 hypothesis sentences along with associated inference labels. The table-sentence pairs are divided into development, and three evaluation sets α_1, α_2, and α_3, each containing 200 unique tables along with nine hypothesis sentences equally distributed among three inference labels (ENTAILMENT, CONTRADICTION, and NEUTRAL). α_1 is a conventional evaluation set that is lexically similar to the training data. α_2 has lexically adversarial hypotheses. And α_3 contains domain topics that are not present in the training set. The remaining 1,740 tables with corresponding 16,538 hypotheses serve as a training set. Table 2 describes the inference performance of RoBERTa$_L$ model on INFOTABS dataset. As we can see, the Human Scores are superior to that of RoBERTa$_L$ model trained with TabFact representation. Since the XINFOTABS is translated directly from the INFOTABS, we expect a similar human baseline for XINFOTABS.

Model	dev	α_1	α_2	α_3
Human	**79.78**	**84.04**	**83.88**	**79.33**
Hypo Only	60.51	60.48	48.26	48.89
RoBERTa$_{LARGE}$	77.61	75.06	69.02	64.61

Table 2: Accuracy scores of the *Table as Struct* strategy on XINFOTABS subsets with RoBERTa$_{LARGE}$ model, hypothesis only baseline and majority human agreement results. The first three rows are reproduced from Gupta et al. (2020).

3 Table Representation

Machine translation of tabular data is a challenging task. Tabular data is semi-structured, non-sentential (ungrammatical), and succinct. The tight form of tabular cells provides inadequate context for today's machine translation models, which are primarily designed to handle sentences. Thus, table translation requires additional context and conversion. Furthermore, frequently occurring named entities in tables must be transliterated rather than translated. Figure 1 shows the table translation pipeline. We describe our approach to context addition and handling of named entities in detail in the following subsections §3.1.

3.1 Table Translation Context

There are several ways to represent tables, each with its own set of pros and cons, as detailed below:

Without Context. The most straightforward way to represent a table would be to treat every key (header) and value (cell) as separate entities and then translate them independently. This approach results in poor translations as the models have no context regarding the keys. The key *"Length"* in English in context of *Movies* would correspond to *"durée"*, meaning *duration* in French but in *Object* context, would correspond to *"longueur"*, meaning *size or span*. Thus, context is essential for accurate table translation.

Full Table. Before transferring data from the header and table cells to translation models, one may concentrate and seam each table row using a delimiter such as a colon (":") to separate key from value and a semi-colon (";") to separate rows (Wenhu Chen and Wang, 2020). This method provides full context and completely translates all table cells. However, in practice, this strategy has two major problems:

a. *Length Constraint*: All transformer-based models have a maximum input string length of 512 tokens.[2] Larger tables with tens of rows may not be translated using this approach.[3] In practice, strings longer than 256 tokens have been shown to have inferior translation quality.[4]

b. *Structural Issue*: When a linearized table is directly translated, the delimiter tokens (":" and ";") get randomly shifted. [5] The delimiter counts are also altered. Hence, the translation appears to merge characters from adjacent rows, resulting in inseparable translations. Ideally, the key and value delimiter token locations should be invariant in a successful translation.

Category Context. Given the shortcomings of the previous two methods, we devise a new strategy: we add a *general context* that describes table rows at a high level to each linearized row cell. We leverage the *table category* here, as it offers enough context to grasp the key's meaning. For the key *"Focus"* in Table 1, the category information *Sports* offers enough context to understand its significance in relation to boxing. The context added representation for this key-value pair will be *"Sports | Focus | Punching , Striking"*. We use "|" delimiter for separating the context, key, and value. Furthermore, multiple values are seperated by ",". Unlike full table translation, row structure is preserved since each row is translated independently and no row surpasses the maximum token limit. We observe an average increase of 5.5% in translation performance (cf. §4).

3.2 Handling Named Entities

Commercial translation methods, like Google Translate, correctly transliterate specified entities (such as proper nouns and dates). However, modern open-source models like mBART50 and M2M100 translate name entity labels, lowering overall translation quality. For example, *Alice Sheets* is translated to *Alice draps* in French. We propose a simple preprocessing technique to address the transliterate/translate ambiguity. First, we use the Named Entity Recognition (NER) model[6](Jiang et al., 2016) to identify entity information that must be transliterated, such as proper nouns and dates. Then, we add a unique identifier in the form

[2] Recently, models bigger than 512 tokens have been developed, e.g. (Asaadi et al., 2019; Beltagy et al., 2020), but no publicly accessible long-sequence (> 512 tokens) multilingual machine translation model exists at the moment. [3] Average # of rows in InfoTabS is: 8.8 for Train, Development, α_1 and α_2, and 13.1 for α_3. [4] Neeraja et al. (2021) raises a similar issue for NLI. [5] Using "|" instead of ":" helps key-value separation. [6] spaCy NER tagger

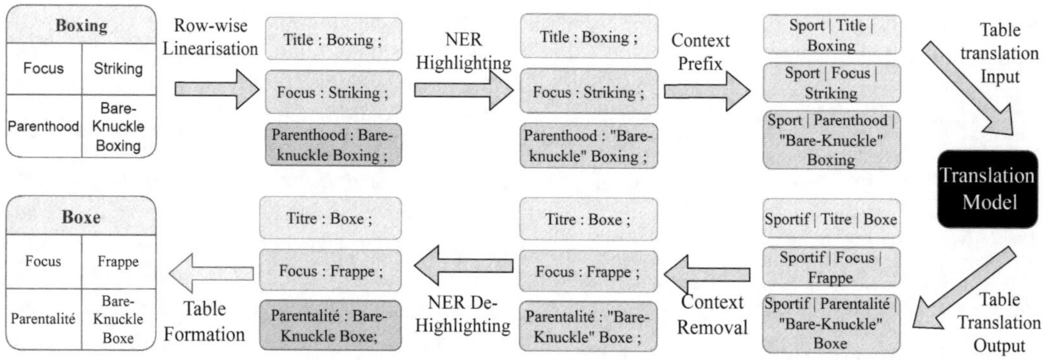

Figure 1: Table translation pipeline (§3) with premise table "Boxing" (from INFOTABS) translated into French.

of double quotations (" "), e.g., *"Alice Sheets"*, and apply the translation model. Finally, we delete the quotation mark (" ") from the translated sentence after it has been translated. This helps the models identify these entities easily due to their pre-training.

4 Translation and Verification

As mentioned previously, we now grasp how to represent a table. Consequently, these reformatted tables can now be fed into reliable translation models. To accomplish this, we assess many prominent multilingual (e.g., mBART50 (Tang et al., 2020) and M2M100 (Fan et al., 2020b)) and bilingual (e.g., MarianMT (Junczys-Dowmunt et al., 2018)) translation models as described below:

Multilingual Models. This category of models used includes widely used machine translation models trained on a large number of languages such as mBART50 (Tang et al., 2020) which can perform translation between any two languages from the list of 50 languages and M2M100 (Fan et al., 2020b) which has 100 training languages. Apart from these models, we used Google Translate[7] to compare against our dataset translation quality.

Bilingual Models. Earlier studies have revealed that bilingual models outperform multilingual models in machine translation of high-resource languages. Thus, for our experiments, we also considered language-specific bilingual translation models in MarianMT (Junczys-Dowmunt et al., 2018) repository. Because the MarianMT models were not available for a few languages (e.g., Korean (ko)) of XINFOTABS, we could not conduct experiments for some languages.

We also use an efficient data sampling technique to determine the ideal translation model for each language, as detailed in the next section. The results for the translations are shown in Table 3.

4.1 Translation Model Selection

Translating the complete INFOTABS dataset to find the optimal model is practically infeasible. Thus, we select a representative subset of the dataset that approximates the full dataset rather well. Finally, we use optimal models to translate the complete INFOTABS dataset. The method used for making the subset is discussed in the ***Table Subset Sampling Strategy*** and ***Hypothesis Subset Sampling Strategy*** sections given below:-

Table Subset Sampling Strategy: In a table, keys can serve as an excellent depiction of the type of data included therein. For example, if the key *"children"* is used, the associated value is almost always a valid *Noun Phrase* or a collection of them. Additionally, the type of keys for a given category remains constant across tables, but the values are always different.[8] This fact is used to sample a subset of diverse tables based on keys and categories. Specifically, we sample tables for each category based on the frequency of occurrence of keys in the dataset to guarantee diversity. The sum of the frequencies of all the keys in a table is computed for each table. Finally, the top 10% of tables with the largest frequency sum in each category are chosen to be included in the subset. In the end, we construct a subset with 11.14% tables yet containing 90.2% of the all unique keys.

Hypothesis Subset Sampling Strategy: To get a diverse subset of hypotheses, we employ Top2Vec (Angelov, 2020) embedding for each

[7] `https://translate.google.co.in/`

[8] There are 2,163 unique keys in INFOTABS.

hypothesis, then use k-means clustering (Jin and Han, 2010) to choose 10% of each cluster. Sampling from each cluster ensures we cover all topics discussed in the hypothesis, resulting in a subset of 2,569 hypothesis texts.

Model Selection Strategy: To choose the translation model that will be used to generate the language datasets, we first translate the premise and hypothesis subsets for all languages using each of the existing models, as described before. Following translation, we compute the various scores detailed in Section 4.2. Finally, the model with the highest average of premise and hypothesis translation ***Human Evaluation Score*** for the specified language is chosen to translate the complete INFOTABS datasets.

4.2 Translation Quality Verification

With the emergence of Transformer-based pre-trained models, significant progress has been made in automated quality assessment using semantic similarity and human sense correlation (Cer et al., 2017) for machine translation evaluation. To verify our created dataset XINFOTABS, we use three automated metrics in addition to human ratings.

Paraphrase Score (PS). PS indicates the amount of information retained from the translated text. To capture this, we estimate the cosine similarity between the original INFOTABS text and the back-translated English XINFOTABS text sentence encodings. We utilize the all-mpnet-v2(Song et al., 2020) model trained using SBERT (Reimers and Gurevych, 2019) method for sentence encoding.

Multilingual Paraphrase Score (mPS). Different from PS, mPS directly uses the multilingual XINFOTABS text instead of the English back-translated text to compare with INFOTABS text. We produce sentence encodings for multilingual semantic similarity using the multilingual-mpnet-base-v2 model (Reimers and Gurevych, 2020) trained using the SBERT method.

BERTScore (BS). BERTScore is an automatic score that shows high human correlation and has been a widely used quality estimation metric for machine translation tasks (Zhang et al., 2019).

Human Evaluation Score (HES) We hired five annotators to label sampled subsets of 500 examples per model and language. Human verification is accomplished by supplying sentence pairs and requesting that annotators classify them as identical or dissimilar based on the meaning expressed by the sentences. For more details, refer to the Appendix §A.

Analysis. We arrive at an average language score of 85 for tables and 91 for hypotheses for the final selected models in all languages. The results are summarised in Table 3. These results are also utilized to determine the optimal models for translating the entire dataset. MarianMT is used to create the entire dataset in German, French, and Spanish, mBART50 is used to create the Tables dataset in Afrikaans, Korean, Hindi, and Arabic, and M2M100 is used to create the entire dataset in Russian and Chinese, as well as the hypothesis dataset in Afrikaans, Korean, Hindi, and Arabic.

5 Experiment and Analysis

In this section, we study the task of Multilingual Tabular NLI, utilizing our XINFOTABS dataset as the benchmark for a variety of multilingual models with multiple training-testing strategies. By doing so, we aim to assess the capacity and cross-lingual transferability of state-of-the-art multilingual models. For the inference task, we linearize the table using the *"Table as Struct"-TabFact* described in INFOTABS.

Multilingual Models: We use pre-trained multilingual models for all our inference label prediction experiments. We use a multilingual mBERT-base (cased) (Devlin et al., 2019) model pre-trained on masked language modeling. This model will be referred to as $\text{mBERT}_{\text{BASE}}$. The other model we evaluated is the XLM-RoBERTa Large (XNLI) model (Conneau et al., 2020), which is trained on masked language modeling and then finetuned for the NLI task using the XNLI dataset. This model is referred to as XLM-R Large (XNLI). For details on hyperparameters, refer to Appendix §B.

Tables 4, 6, and 7 show the performance of the discussed multilingual models for α_1, α_2, and α_3 test splits respectively. Tables 6 and 7 are shown in Appendix §C, due to limited space. On all three evaluation sets, regardless of task type, the $\text{XLM-RoBERTa}_{\text{Large}}$ model outperforms mBERT. This might be because XLM-RoBERTa has more parameters, and is better pre-trained and pre-tuned for the NLI task using the XNLI dataset.

Model	Metric	de	fr	es	af	ru	zh	ko	hi	ar	MdlAvg
MarianMT	PS	95 I 96	93 I 95	93 I 96	83 I 88	81 I 87	75 I 85	N.A.	56 I 55	60 I 79	80 I 85
	mPS	92 I 95	87 I 96	90 I 96	83 I 84	78 I 84	79 I 83	N.A.	65 I 64	66 I 74	80 I 85
	BS	93 I 94	91 I 94	92 I 94	84 I 89	81 I 87	73 I 85	N.A.	63 I 68	64 I 83	80 I 87
	HES	95 I 87	92 I 86	92 I 94	70 I 56	84 I 54	75 I 59	N.A.	40 I 23	58 I 56	76 I 64
	LnAvg	**94** I 93	**91** I 93	**92** I 95	80 I 79	81 I 78	76 I 78	N.A.	56 I 53	62 I 73	79 I 80
mBART50	PS	94 I 96	93 I 95	86 I 87	88 I 92	89 I 87	81 I 87	83 I 82	85 I 82	70 I 77	85 I 87
	mPS	92 I 96	90 I 96	72 I 92	85 I 91	81 I 88	79 I 84	86 I 83	79 I 81	80 I 80	83 I 88
	BS	91 I 94	91 I 93	71 I 88	88 I 93	85 I 89	77 I 86	79 I 85	82 I 86	76 I 83	82 I 89
	HES	93 I 84	91 I 81	82 I 80	89 I 69	87 I 69	76 I 61	76 I 54	79 I 70	71 I 53	83 I 69
	LnAvg	93 I 93	91 I 91	78 I 87	**88** I 86	86 I 83	78 I 80	**81** I 76	**81** I 80	**74** I 73	83 I 83
M2M100	PS	89 I 96	92 I 94	88 I 95	91 I 94	89 I 90	83 I 82	83 I 92	83 I 88	72 I 77	86 I 90
	mPS	88 I 96	88 I 96	88 I 96	84 I 92	83 I 88	80 I 86	84 I 90	81 I 87	78 I 92	84 I 91
	BS	87 I 94	89 I 93	86 I 93	89 I 94	87 I 90	81 I 88	80 I 90	81 I 89	73 I 88	84 I 91
	HES	88 I 85	86 I 86	84 I 86	86 I 83	87 I 74	79 I 72	70 I 82	75 I 73	60 I 51	79 I 77
	LnAvg	88 I 93	89 I 92	87 I 93	88 I 91	**87** I 86	**81** I 82	79 I 89	80 I 84	71 I 77	83 I 87
GoogleTr	PS	91 I 94	94 I 93	92 I 93	96 I 95	79 I 86	80 I 83	87 I 89	90 I 85	60 I 81	85 I 89
	mPS	89 I 94	88 I 94	88 I 94	82 I 87	82 I 86	80 I 86	83 I 87	77 I 80	71 I 81	82 I 88
	BS	87 I 91	89 I 90	88 I 91	88 I 93	77 I 85	78 I 82	82 I 85	87 I 85	63 I 82	82 I 87
	HES	91 I 79	93 I 81	89 I 83	96 I 81	84 I 66	79 I 56	79 I 70	92 I 74	65 I 70	85 I 73
	LnAvg	90 I 90	91 I 90	89 I 90	91 I 89	81 I 81	79 I 77	83 I 83	87 I 81	65 I 79	84 I 84

Table 3: Table translation experiment results with Paraphrase Score (PS), Multilingual Paraphrase Score (mPS), BERTScore (BS), Human Evaluation Score (HES), Language Average (LnAvg) and Model Average (MdlAvg). We use the "X I Y" format, where X and Y represent the Table and hypothesis translation score respectively. **Purple** and Orange signifies the language average score of the model selected for table and hypothesis translation respectively.

5.1 Using English Translated Test Sets

We aim to investigate the following question: *How would models trained on original English* INFOTABS *perform on English translated multilingual* XINFOTABS*?*. We trained multilingual models using the original English INFOTABS training set, and used the English translated XINFOTABS development set, and three test sets during the evaluation. According to Table 4, German has the best language-wise performance for α_1. From Table 6, German, French, and Afrikaans have the highest average scores for α_2. French and Russian have the best scores on α_3 as shown in Table 7. Arabic has the lowest average of any language across all three test sets. Here, the model trained on English INFOTABS is being used for all the languages. Since the model is the same for all languages, the variation in performance only depends on English translation across XINFOTABS languages. On α_2 and α_3 sets, this task on average performs competitively against all other baseline tasks.

5.2 Language-Specific Model Training

In this subsection, we try to answer the question: *Is it beneficial to train a language-specific model on* XINFOTABS*?* In doing so, we finetune ten distinct models, one for each language on XINFOTABS. Comparing models on this task helps comprehend the model's intrinsic multilingual capabilities for tabular reasoning. Among the language-specific models, English has the best language average in all three test sets, while Arabic has the lowest.

Additionally, there is a substantial variation in the quality of translation and model multilingualism competence. The high-resource languages often perform better since the pre-trained models have been trained on a larger amount of data from these languages. Surprisingly, §5.2 setting has lower average mBERT scores for all three splits than §5.1 setting. The benefit of training the model in English seems to surpass any loss incurred during translating test sets into English. However, this is not the case with XLM-R(XNLI). The average scores increase substantially for α_1 split in §5.2 setting compared to §5.1 setting, decrease slightly for α_2, and remain constant for α_3. The α_1 set improves due to its similar split to the train set, whereas the α_2 set slightly worsens since it includes human-annotated perturbed hypotheses with labels flipped. Lastly, the α_3 set comprises tables from zero-shot domains i.e. unseen domain tables, so it remains constant. Our exploration of models' cross-lingual transferability is provided in Appendix§ D.

5.3 Fine-tuning on Multiple Languages

Earlier findings indicate that fine-tuning multilingual models for the same task across

Train/Test Strategy	Model	en	de	fr	es	af	ru	zh	ko	hi	ar	Model. Avg.
English Translated Test (§5.1)	mBERT$_{BASE}$	-	66	64	65	66	63	63	64	64	59	64
	XLM-R$_{LARGE}$ (XNLI)	-	73	73	72	72	72	71	69	70	62	70
	Lang. Avg.	-	70	69	69	69	67	67	67	67	61	68
Language Specific Training (§5.2)	mBERT$_{BASE}$	67	65	65	63	62	64	63	61	63	57	63
	XLM-R$_{LARGE}$ (XNLI)	76	75	74	74	72	71	73	71	71	68	72
	Lang. Avg.	72	70	69	68	67	67	68	66	67	63	68
Multiple Language Finetuning Using Only English (§5.3A)	mBERT$_{BASE}$	-	64	66	64	64	64	65	63	62	62	64
	XLM-R$_{LARGE}$ (XNLI)	-	75	74	75	74	74	73	73	72	69	73
	Lang. Avg.	-	69	70	69	69	69	69	68	67	66	**69**
Multiple Language Finetuning Unified Model (§5.3B)	mBERT$_{BASE}$	65	64	64	64	64	63	64	62	62	59	63
	XLM-R$_{LARGE}$ (XNLI)	76	75	74	75	73	74	74	73	72	70	74
	Lang. Avg.	71	69	69	70	69	68	69	67	67	65	**69**
English Premise Multilingual Hypothesis (§5.4)	mBERT$_{BASE}$	-	63	63	64	62	61	61	59	61	60	61
	XLM-R$_{LARGE}$ (XNLI)	-	73	73	73	72	72	73	72	71	68	72
	Lang. Avg.	-	68	68	68	67	67	67	66	66	64	67

Table 4: Accuracy for baseline tasks on the α_1 set. **Purple** signifies the best task average accuracy, Orange signifies the best language average accuracy, Cerulean signifies the best model accuracy. XLM-R$_{LARGE}$ represent XLM-RoBERTa$_{LARGE}$ model.

languages improves performance in the target language (Phang et al., 2020; Wang et al., 2019; Pruksachatkun et al., 2020). Thus, *do models benefit from sequential fine-tuning over several* XINFOTABS *languages?* To answer it, we investigate this strategy of pre-finetuning in two ways, (a) by using English as the predominant language for pre-finetuning, and (b) by utilizing all XINFOTABS languages to train a unified model, .

A. Using English Language. We fine-tune our models on the English INFOTABS and then on XINFOTABS in each language individually. Thus, we train nine models in total, one for each multilingual language (except English). English was chosen as the pre-finetuning language due to its strong performance in the §5.2 paradigm and prior research demonstrating English's superior cross-lingual transfer capacity (Phang et al., 2020). Across all three splits, the average score improves from the §5.2 setting, demonstrating that pre-finetuning the English dataset benefits other multilingual languages. The most significant gains are shown in lower resource languages, notably Arabic, which improved by 3% for α_1, 2% for α_2, and 1% for α_3 in comparison to the §5.2 approach.

B. Unified Model Approach. We explore whether fine-tuning on other languages is beneficial, where we fine-tune a single unified model across all XINFOTABS languages' training sets and use it for making predictions on XINFOTABS test sets. We observe that the finetuning language order affects the final model performance if done sequentially. We find that training from a high to a low resource language leads to the highest average accuracy improvement. This is due to the catastrophic forgetting trait (Goodfellow et al., 2015), which encourages training on more straightforward examples first, i.e., those with better performance. Hence, we trained in the following language order: en $\rightarrow$ fr $\rightarrow$ de $\rightarrow$ es $\rightarrow$ af $\rightarrow$ ru $\rightarrow$ zh $\rightarrow$ hi$\rightarrow$ ko $\rightarrow$ ar.

We observe that the XLM RoBERTa Large model performs the best across all baseline tasks in the α_1 set. On average, this performance is comparable to English pre-finetuning. While the accuracy of high resource languages remains constant or marginally declines compared to the §5.2 setting, there is a substantial improvement in accuracy for low resource languages, particularly Arabic, which increases by 2%. It performs similarly to English pre-finetuning. To conclude, more fine-tuning is not always beneficial for all models, but it benefits larger models like the XLM-R Large. Models improve performance for low-resource languages compared to the §5.2 setting (i.e., no pre-finetuning), but not nearly as much as that of English-based pre-finetuning.

5.4 English Premise Multilingual Hypothesis

The premise of English's multilingual hypothesis is practical, as it is frequently observed in the real world. The majority of the world's facts and information are written in English. For instance, Wikipedia has more tables in English than in any other language, and even if a page is available, it is likely that it missing an infobox. However, because people are innately bilingual, inquiries or verification queries concerning these facts could be in a language other than English. As a result, the task of developing cross-lingual tabular NLI is critical in the real world.

To study this problem, we look at the following question: *How effective are models with premise and hypothesis stated in distinct languages?* To answer this, we train the models using the original INFOTABS premise tables in the English language and multilingual hypotheses in XINFOTABS, i.e., nine languages. We note that XLM-R Large (XNLI) has the highest accuracy for the α_1 set. On average, the high-resource languages German, French, and Spanish perform favorably across models, whereas Arabic underperforms. Both models have shallow scores in German for the α_2 set, which defy earlier observations. This might be because the adversarial modifications in the α_2 hypothesis might not be reflected in the German translation. XLM-R Large has the highest accuracy on this set, with French and Spanish being the most accurate languages. The models for the α_3 validation set demonstrate that language average accuracy is nearly proportional to the size of translation resources. However, the scores are marginally lower on average for the α_2 set.

Surprisingly, models perform worse on average than with §5.2 setting on the α_1 and α_2 sets while performing similarly on the α_3 set. Except for α_2 on German, the average language accuracy changes are directly proportional to the language resource, implying that the constraint could be translation quality; left for future study. Refer Appendix §E for robustness and consistency analysis.

6 Discussion and Analysis

Extraction vs. Translation. One straightforward idea for constructing the multilingual tabular NLI dataset is to extract multilingual tables from Wikipedia in the considered languages. However, this strategy fails in practice for several reasons. For starters, not all articles are multilingual. For example, only 750 of the 2540 tables were from articles available in Hindi. The existence of the same title articles across several languages does not indicate that the tables are identical. Only 500 of the 750 tables with articles in Hindi had infoboxes, and most of these tables were considerably different from the English tables. The tables had different numbers of keys and different value information.

Human Verification vs. Human Translation. We selected machine translation with human verification over hiring expert translators for several reasons: (a) Hiring bilingual, skilled translators in multiple languages is expensive and challenging, (b) Human verification is a more straightforward classification task based on semantic similarity; it is also less erroneous compared to translation, (c) By selecting an appropriate verification sample size, we may further minimize the time and effort required for human inspection, (d) A competent translation system has no effect on the classification labels used in inference. As a result, the loss of the semantic connection between the table and the hypothesis is not a significant issue (K et al., 2021), and (e) Minor translation errors have no effect on the downstream NLI task label as long as the semantic meaning of the translation is retained (Conneau et al., 2018; K et al., 2021; Cohn-Gordon and Goodman, 2019; Carl, 2000).

Usage and Future Direction. The dataset can be used to test benchmarks, multilingual models, and methods for tabular NLI. In addition to language invariance, robustness, and multilingual fact verification, it may well be utilized for reasoning tasks like multilingual question answering (Demszky et al., 2018). The baselines can also be beneficial to understand models' cross-lingual transferability.

Our current table structure does not generate natural language sentences and hence does not optimize the capabilities of a machine translation model. The representation of tables can be enhanced further by adding Better Paragraph Representation (BPR) from Neeraja et al. (2021). Additionally, NER handling may be enhanced by inserting a predetermined template name into the sentence post-translation, i.e. extracting a named entity from the original sentence, replacing it with a fixed template entity, and then replacing the named entity with the template post-translation. Multiple experiments, however, would be necessary to identify suitable template entities for replacement, and hence this is left as future work. Another approach is the extraction of keys and values from multilingual Wikipedia pages is also a challenging task and left as future work. Finally, human intervention can enhance the translation quality by either direct human translation or fine-grained post-translation verification and correction.

7 Related Work

Tabular Reasoning. Recent studies investigate various NLP tasks on semi-structured tabular data, including tabular NLI and fact verification (Chen et al., 2019; Gupta et al., 2020; Zhang and Balog, 2019), tabular probing (Gupta et al., 2021), various question answering and semantic parsing tasks (Pasupat and Liang, 2015; Krishnamurthy et al., 2017; Abbas et al., 2016; Sun et al., 2016; Chen et al., 2020b; Lin et al., 2020; Zayats et al., 2021; Oguz et al., 2020; Chen et al., 2021, *inter alia*), and table-to-text generation (e.g., Parikh et al., 2020; Nan et al., 2021; Yoran et al., 2021; Chen et al., 2020a). Several strategies for representing Wikipedia relational tables were recently proposed, such as TAPAS (Herzig et al., 2020), TaBERT (Yin et al., 2020), TabStruc (Zhang et al., 2020), TABBIE (Iida et al., 2021), TabGCN (Pramanick and Bhattacharya, 2021) and RCI (Glass et al., 2021). Yu et al. (2018, 2021); Eisenschlos et al. (2020) and Neeraja et al. (2021) study pre-training for improving tabular inference.

Multilingual Datasets and Models. Given the need for greater inclusivity towards linguistic diversity in NLP applications, various multilingual versions of datasets have been created for text classification (Conneau et al., 2018; Yang et al., 2019; Ponti et al., 2020), question answering (Lewis et al., 2020; Clark et al., 2020; Artetxe et al., 2020) and structure prediction (Rahimi et al., 2019; Nivre et al., 2016). Following the introduction of datasets, multilingual leaderboards like XTREME leaderboard (Hu et al., 2020), the XGLUE leaderboard (Liang et al., 2020) and the XTREME-R leaderboard (Ruder et al., 2021) have been created to test models' cross-lingual transfer and language understanding.

Multilingual models can be broadly classified into two variants: (a) Natural Language Understanding (NLU) models like mBERT (Devlin et al., 2019), XLM (Conneau and Lample, 2019), XLM-R (Conneau et al., 2020), XLM-E (Chi et al., 2021), RemBERT (Chung et al., 2021), and (b) Natural Language Generation (NLG) models like mT5 (Xue et al., 2021), mBART (Liu et al., 2020), M2M100 (Fan et al., 2021). NLU models have been used in multilingual language understanding tasks like sentiment analysis, semantic similarity and natural language inference while NLG models are used in generation tasks like question-answering and machine translation.

Machine Translation. Modern machine translation models involve having an encoder-decoder generator model trained on either bilingual (Tran et al., 2021) or a multilingual parallel corpus with monolingual pre-training e.g. mBART (Liu et al., 2020) and M2M100 (Fan et al., 2021). These models have been shown to work very well even for low-resource languages due to cross-language transfer properties. Recently auxiliary pertaining for machine translation models have garnered attention, with a focus on autonomous quality estimation metrics (Specia et al., 2018; Fonseca et al., 2019; Specia et al., 2020). As such, automatic scores like the BERTScore (Zhang et al., 2019), Bleurt (Sellam et al., 2020) and COMET Score (Rei et al., 2020) have high human evaluation correlation, are increasingly used to assess NLG tasks.

8 Conclusion

We built the first multilingual tabular NLI dataset, namely XINFOTABS, by expanding the INFOTABS dataset with ten different languages. This is accomplished by our novel machine translation approach for tables, which yields remarkable results in practice. We thoroughly evaluated our translation quality to demonstrate that the dataset meets the acceptable standard. We further examined the performance of multiple multilingual models on three validation sets of varying difficulty, with methods ranging from the basic translation-based technique to more complicated language-specific and intermediate task finetuning. Our results demonstrate that, despite the models' success, this dataset remains a difficult challenge for multilingual inference. Lastly, we gave a thorough error analysis of the models to comprehend their cross-linguistic transferability, robustness to language change, and coherence with reasoning.

Acknowledgement

We thank members of the Utah NLP group for their valuable insights and suggestions at various stages of the project; and reviewers their helpful comments. Additionally, we appreciate the inputs provided by Vivek Srikumar and Ellen Riloff. Vivek Gupta acknowledges support from Bloomberg's Data Science Ph.D. Fellowship.

References

Faheem Abbas, M. K. Malik, M. Rashid, and Rizwan Zafar. 2016. Wikiqa — a question answering system on wikipedia using freebase, dbpedia and infobox. *2016 Sixth International Conference on Innovative Computing Technology (INTECH)*, pages 185–193.

Dimo Angelov. 2020. Top2vec: Distributed representations of topics.

Mikel Artetxe, Sebastian Ruder, and Dani Yogatama. 2020. On the cross-lingual transferability of monolingual representations. In *Proceedings of the 58th Annual Meeting of the Association for Computational Linguistics*, pages 4623–4637, Online. Association for Computational Linguistics.

Shima Asaadi, Saif Mohammad, and Svetlana Kiritchenko. 2019. Big BiRD: A large, fine-grained, bigram relatedness dataset for examining semantic composition. In *Proceedings of the 2019 Conference of the North American Chapter of the Association for Computational Linguistics: Human Language Technologies, Volume 1 (Long and Short Papers)*, pages 505–516, Minneapolis, Minnesota. Association for Computational Linguistics.

Iz Beltagy, Matthew E. Peters, and Arman Cohan. 2020. Longformer: The long-document transformer. *CoRR*, abs/2004.05150.

Michael Carl. 2000. On the meaning preservation capacities in machine translation.

Daniel Cer, Mona Diab, Eneko Agirre, Iñigo Lopez-Gazpio, and Lucia Specia. 2017. SemEval-2017 task 1: Semantic textual similarity multilingual and crosslingual focused evaluation. In *Proceedings of the 11th International Workshop on Semantic Evaluation (SemEval-2017)*, pages 1–14, Vancouver, Canada. Association for Computational Linguistics.

Wenhu Chen, Ming-Wei Chang, Eva Schlinger, William Yang Wang, and William W. Cohen. 2021. Open question answering over tables and text. In *International Conference on Learning Representations*.

Wenhu Chen, Jianshu Chen, Yu Su, Zhiyu Chen, and William Yang Wang. 2020a. Logical natural language generation from open-domain tables. In *Proceedings of the 58th Annual Meeting of the Association for Computational Linguistics*, pages 7929–7942, Online. Association for Computational Linguistics.

Wenhu Chen, Hongmin Wang, Jianshu Chen, Yunkai Zhang, Hong Wang, Shiyang Li, Xiyou Zhou, and William Yang Wang. 2019. Tabfact: A large-scale dataset for table-based fact verification. In *International Conference on Learning Representations*.

Wenhu Chen, Hanwen Zha, Zhiyu Chen, Wenhan Xiong, Hong Wang, and William Yang Wang. 2020b. HybridQA: A dataset of multi-hop question answering over tabular and textual data. In *Findings of the Association for Computational Linguistics: EMNLP 2020*, pages 1026–1036, Online. Association for Computational Linguistics.

Zewen Chi, Shaohan Huang, Li Dong, Shuming Ma, Saksham Singhal, Payal Bajaj, Xia Song, and Furu Wei. 2021. Xlm-e: Cross-lingual language model pre-training via electra. *CoRR*, abs/2106.16138.

Hyung Won Chung, Thibault Fevry, Henry Tsai, Melvin Johnson, and Sebastian Ruder. 2021. Rethinking embedding coupling in pre-trained language models. In *International Conference on Learning Representations*.

Jonathan H. Clark, Eunsol Choi, Michael Collins, Dan Garrette, Tom Kwiatkowski, Vitaly Nikolaev, and Jennimaria Palomaki. 2020. TyDi QA: A benchmark for information-seeking question answering in typologically diverse languages. *Transactions of the Association for Computational Linguistics*, 8:454–470.

Reuben Cohn-Gordon and Noah D. Goodman. 2019. Lost in machine translation: A method to reduce meaning loss. *CoRR*, abs/1902.09514.

Alexis Conneau, Kartikay Khandelwal, Naman Goyal, Vishrav Chaudhary, Guillaume Wenzek, Francisco Guzmán, Edouard Grave, Myle Ott, Luke Zettlemoyer, and Veselin Stoyanov. 2020. Unsupervised cross-lingual representation learning at scale. In *Proceedings of the 58th Annual Meeting of the Association for Computational Linguistics*, pages 8440–8451, Online. Association for Computational Linguistics.

Alexis Conneau and Guillaume Lample. 2019. Cross-lingual language model pretraining. *Advances in Neural Information Processing Systems*, 32:7059–7069.

Alexis Conneau, Ruty Rinott, Guillaume Lample, Adina Williams, Samuel Bowman, Holger Schwenk, and Veselin Stoyanov. 2018. XNLI: Evaluating cross-lingual sentence representations. In *Proceedings of the 2018 Conference on Empirical Methods in Natural Language Processing*, pages 2475–2485, Brussels, Belgium. Association for Computational Linguistics.

Dorottya Demszky, Kelvin Guu, and Percy Liang. 2018. Transforming question answering datasets into natural language inference datasets. *arXiv preprint arXiv:1809.02922*.

Jacob Devlin, Ming-Wei Chang, Kenton Lee, and Kristina Toutanova. 2019. BERT: Pre-training of Deep Bidirectional Transformers for Language Understanding. In *Proceedings of the 2019 Conference of the North American Chapter of the Association for Computational Linguistics: Human Language Technologies*.

Julian Eisenschlos, Syrine Krichene, and Thomas Müller. 2020. Understanding tables with intermediate pre-training. In *Findings of the Association for Computational Linguistics: EMNLP 2020*, pages 281–296, Online. Association for Computational Linguistics.

Angela Fan, Shruti Bhosale, Holger Schwenk, Zhiyi Ma, Ahmed El-Kishky, Siddharth Goyal, Mandeep Baines, Onur Celebi, Guillaume Wenzek, Vishrav Chaudhary, Naman Goyal, Tom Birch, Vitaliy Liptchinsky, Sergey Edunov, Edouard Grave, Michael Auli, and Armand Joulin. 2020a. Beyond english-centric multilingual machine translation. *arXiv preprint*.

Angela Fan, Shruti Bhosale, Holger Schwenk, Zhiyi Ma, Ahmed El-Kishky, Siddharth Goyal, Mandeep Baines, Onur Celebi, Guillaume Wenzek, Vishrav Chaudhary, Naman Goyal, Tom Birch, Vitaliy Liptchinsky, Sergey Edunov, Edouard Grave, Michael Auli, and Armand Joulin. 2020b. Beyond english-centric multilingual machine translation.

Angela Fan, Shruti Bhosale, Holger Schwenk, Zhiyi Ma, Ahmed El-Kishky, Siddharth Goyal, Mandeep Baines, Onur Celebi, Guillaume Wenzek, Vishrav Chaudhary, et al. 2021. Beyond english-centric multilingual machine translation. *Journal of Machine Learning Research*, 22(107):1–48.

Erick Fonseca, Lisa Yankovskaya, André F. T. Martins, Mark Fishel, and Christian Federmann. 2019. Findings of the WMT 2019 shared tasks on quality estimation. In *Proceedings of the Fourth Conference on Machine Translation (Volume 3: Shared Task Papers, Day 2)*, pages 1–10, Florence, Italy. Association for Computational Linguistics.

Michael Glass, Mustafa Canim, Alfio Gliozzo, Saneem Chemmengath, Vishwajeet Kumar, Rishav Chakravarti, Avi Sil, Feifei Pan, Samarth Bharadwaj, and Nicolas Rodolfo Fauceglia. 2021. Capturing row and column semantics in transformer based question answering over tables. In *Proceedings of the 2021 Conference of the North American Chapter of the Association for Computational Linguistics: Human Language Technologies*, pages 1212–1224, Online. Association for Computational Linguistics.

Ian J. Goodfellow, Mehdi Mirza, Da Xiao, Aaron Courville, and Yoshua Bengio. 2015. An empirical investigation of catastrophic forgetting in gradient-based neural networks.

Vivek Gupta, Riyaz A Bhat, Atreya Ghosal, Manish Srivastava, Maneesh Singh, and Vivek Srikumar. 2021. Is my model using the right evidence? systematic probes for examining evidence-based tabular reasoning. *arXiv preprint arXiv:2108.00578*.

Vivek Gupta, Maitrey Mehta, Pegah Nokhiz, and Vivek Srikumar. 2020. INFOTABS: Inference on tables as semi-structured data. In *Proceedings of the 58th Annual Meeting of the Association for Computational Linguistics*, pages 2309–2324, Online. Association for Computational Linguistics.

Jonathan Herzig, Pawel Krzysztof Nowak, Thomas Müller, Francesco Piccinno, and Julian Eisenschlos. 2020. TaPas: Weakly supervised table parsing via pre-training. In *Proceedings of the 58th Annual Meeting of the Association for Computational Linguistics*, pages 4320–4333, Online. Association for Computational Linguistics.

Junjie Hu, Sebastian Ruder, Aditya Siddhant, Graham Neubig, Orhan Firat, and Melvin Johnson. 2020. Xtreme: A massively multilingual multi-task benchmark for evaluating cross-lingual generalisation. In *International Conference on Machine Learning*, pages 4411–4421. PMLR.

Hiroshi Iida, Dung Thai, Varun Manjunatha, and Mohit Iyyer. 2021. TABBIE: Pretrained representations of tabular data. In *Proceedings of the 2021 Conference of the North American Chapter of the Association for Computational Linguistics: Human Language Technologies*, pages 3446–3456, Online. Association for Computational Linguistics.

Ridong Jiang, Rafael E. Banchs, and Haizhou Li. 2016. Evaluating and combining name entity recognition systems. In *Proceedings of the Sixth Named Entity Workshop*, pages 21–27, Berlin, Germany. Association for Computational Linguistics.

Xin Jin and Jiawei Han. 2010. *K-Means Clustering*, pages 563–564. Springer US, Boston, MA.

Marcin Junczys-Dowmunt, Roman Grundkiewicz, Tomasz Dwojak, Hieu Hoang, Kenneth Heafield, Tom Neckermann, Frank Seide, Ulrich Germann, Alham Fikri Aji, Nikolay Bogoychev, André F. T. Martins, and Alexandra Birch. 2018. Marian: Fast neural machine translation in C++. In *Proceedings of ACL 2018, System Demonstrations*, pages 116–121, Melbourne, Australia. Association for Computational Linguistics.

Karthikeyan K, Aalok Sathe, Somak Aditya, and Monojit Choudhury. 2021. Analyzing the effects of reasoning types on cross-lingual transfer performance. In *Proceedings of the 1st Workshop on Multilingual Representation Learning*, pages 86–95, Punta Cana, Dominican Republic. Association for Computational Linguistics.

Philipp Koehn and Christof Monz. 2006. Manual and automatic evaluation of machine translation between European languages. In *Proceedings on the Workshop on Statistical Machine Translation*, pages 102–121, New York City. Association for Computational Linguistics.

Jayant Krishnamurthy, Pradeep Dasigi, and Matt Gardner. 2017. Neural semantic parsing with type constraints for semi-structured tables. In *Proceedings of the 2017 Conference on Empirical Methods in Natural Language Processing*, pages

1516–1526, Copenhagen, Denmark. Association for Computational Linguistics.

Patrick Lewis, Barlas Oguz, Ruty Rinott, Sebastian Riedel, and Holger Schwenk. 2020. MLQA: Evaluating cross-lingual extractive question answering. In *Proceedings of the 58th Annual Meeting of the Association for Computational Linguistics*, pages 7315–7330, Online. Association for Computational Linguistics.

Xiaoyu Li and Francesco Orabona. 2019. On the convergence of stochastic gradient descent with adaptive stepsizes. In *The 22nd International Conference on Artificial Intelligence and Statistics*, pages 983–992. PMLR.

Yaobo Liang, Nan Duan, Yeyun Gong, Ning Wu, Fenfei Guo, Weizhen Qi, Ming Gong, Linjun Shou, Daxin Jiang, Guihong Cao, Xiaodong Fan, Ruofei Zhang, Rahul Agrawal, Edward Cui, Sining Wei, Taroon Bharti, Ying Qiao, Jiun-Hung Chen, Winnie Wu, Shuguang Liu, Fan Yang, Daniel Campos, Rangan Majumder, and Ming Zhou. 2020. XGLUE: A new benchmark datasetfor cross-lingual pre-training, understanding and generation. In *Proceedings of the 2020 Conference on Empirical Methods in Natural Language Processing (EMNLP)*, pages 6008–6018, Online. Association for Computational Linguistics.

Xi Victoria Lin, Richard Socher, and Caiming Xiong. 2020. Bridging textual and tabular data for cross-domain text-to-SQL semantic parsing. In *Findings of the Association for Computational Linguistics: EMNLP 2020*, pages 4870–4888, Online. Association for Computational Linguistics.

Yinhan Liu, Jiatao Gu, Naman Goyal, Xian Li, Sergey Edunov, Marjan Ghazvininejad, Mike Lewis, and Luke Zettlemoyer. 2020. Multilingual denoising pre-training for neural machine translation. *Transactions of the Association for Computational Linguistics*, 8:726–742.

Yinhan Liu, Myle Ott, Naman Goyal, Jingfei Du, Mandar Joshi, Danqi Chen, Omer Levy, Mike Lewis, Luke Zettlemoyer, and Veselin Stoyanov. 2019. Roberta: A Robustly Optimized BERT Pretraining Approach. *arXiv preprint arXiv:1907.11692*.

Ilya Loshchilov and Frank Hutter. 2017. Decoupled weight decay regularization. *arXiv preprint arXiv:1711.05101*.

Linyong Nan, Dragomir Radev, Rui Zhang, Amrit Rau, Abhinand Sivaprasad, Chiachun Hsieh, Xiangru Tang, Aadit Vyas, Neha Verma, Pranav Krishna, Yangxiaokang Liu, Nadia Irwanto, Jessica Pan, Faiaz Rahman, Ahmad Zaidi, Mutethia Mutuma, Yasin Tarabar, Ankit Gupta, Tao Yu, Yi Chern Tan, Xi Victoria Lin, Caiming Xiong, Richard Socher, and Nazneen Fatema Rajani. 2021. DART: Open-domain structured data record to text generation. In *Proceedings of the 2021 Conference of the North American Chapter of the Association for Computational Linguistics: Human Language Technologies*, pages 432–447, Online. Association for Computational Linguistics.

J. Neeraja, Vivek Gupta, and Vivek Srikumar. 2021. Incorporating external knowledge to enhance tabular reasoning. In *Proceedings of the 2021 Conference of the North American Chapter of the Association for Computational Linguistics: Human Language Technologies*, pages 2799–2809, Online. Association for Computational Linguistics.

Joakim Nivre, Marie-Catherine de Marneffe, Filip Ginter, Yoav Goldberg, Jan Hajič, Christopher D. Manning, Ryan McDonald, Slav Petrov, Sampo Pyysalo, Natalia Silveira, Reut Tsarfaty, and Daniel Zeman. 2016. Universal Dependencies v1: A multilingual treebank collection. In *Proceedings of the Tenth International Conference on Language Resources and Evaluation (LREC'16)*, pages 1659–1666, Portorož, Slovenia. European Language Resources Association (ELRA).

Barlas Oguz, Xilun Chen, Vladimir Karpukhin, Stan Peshterliev, Dmytro Okhonko, Michael Schlichtkrull, Sonal Gupta, Yashar Mehdad, and Scott Yih. 2020. Unified open-domain question answering with structured and unstructured knowledge. *arXiv preprint arXiv:2012.14610*.

Ankur Parikh, Xuezhi Wang, Sebastian Gehrmann, Manaal Faruqui, Bhuwan Dhingra, Diyi Yang, and Dipanjan Das. 2020. ToTTo: A controlled table-to-text generation dataset. In *Proceedings of the 2020 Conference on Empirical Methods in Natural Language Processing (EMNLP)*, pages 1173–1186, Online. Association for Computational Linguistics.

Panupong Pasupat and Percy Liang. 2015. Compositional semantic parsing on semi-structured tables. In *Proceedings of the 53rd Annual Meeting of the Association for Computational Linguistics and the 7th International Joint Conference on Natural Language Processing (Volume 1: Long Papers)*, pages 1470–1480, Beijing, China. Association for Computational Linguistics.

Jason Phang, Iacer Calixto, Phu Mon Htut, Yada Pruksachatkun, Haokun Liu, Clara Vania, Katharina Kann, and Samuel R. Bowman. 2020. English intermediate-task training improves zero-shot cross-lingual transfer too. In *Proceedings of the 1st Conference of the Asia-Pacific Chapter of the Association for Computational Linguistics and the 10th International Joint Conference on Natural Language Processing*, pages 557–575, Suzhou, China. Association for Computational Linguistics.

Edoardo Maria Ponti, Goran Glavaš, Olga Majewska, Qianchu Liu, Ivan Vulić, and Anna Korhonen. 2020. XCOPA: A multilingual dataset for causal commonsense reasoning. In *Proceedings of the 2020 Conference on Empirical Methods in Natural Language Processing (EMNLP)*, pages 2362–2376, Online. Association for Computational Linguistics.

Aniket Pramanick and Indrajit Bhattacharya. 2021. Joint learning of representations for web-tables, entities and types using graph convolutional network. In *Proceedings of the 16th Conference of the European Chapter of the Association for Computational Linguistics: Main Volume*, pages 1197–1206, Online. Association for Computational Linguistics.

Yada Pruksachatkun, Jason Phang, Haokun Liu, Phu Mon Htut, Xiaoyi Zhang, Richard Yuanzhe Pang, Clara Vania, Katharina Kann, and Samuel R. Bowman. 2020. Intermediate-task transfer learning with pretrained language models: When and why does it work? In *Proceedings of the 58th Annual Meeting of the Association for Computational Linguistics*, pages 5231–5247, Online. Association for Computational Linguistics.

Afshin Rahimi, Yuan Li, and Trevor Cohn. 2019. Massively multilingual transfer for NER. In *Proceedings of the 57th Annual Meeting of the Association for Computational Linguistics*, pages 151–164, Florence, Italy. Association for Computational Linguistics.

Ricardo Rei, Craig Stewart, Ana C Farinha, and Alon Lavie. 2020. COMET: A neural framework for MT evaluation. In *Proceedings of the 2020 Conference on Empirical Methods in Natural Language Processing (EMNLP)*, pages 2685–2702, Online. Association for Computational Linguistics.

Nils Reimers and Iryna Gurevych. 2019. Sentence-bert: Sentence embeddings using siamese bert-networks.

Nils Reimers and Iryna Gurevych. 2020. Making monolingual sentence embeddings multilingual using knowledge distillation. In *Proceedings of the 2020 Conference on Empirical Methods in Natural Language Processing*. Association for Computational Linguistics.

Sebastian Ruder, Noah Constant, Jan Botha, Aditya Siddhant, Orhan Firat, Jinlan Fu, Pengfei Liu, Junjie Hu, Dan Garrette, Graham Neubig, and Melvin Johnson. 2021. XTREME-R: Towards more challenging and nuanced multilingual evaluation. In *Proceedings of the 2021 Conference on Empirical Methods in Natural Language Processing*, pages 10215–10245, Online and Punta Cana, Dominican Republic. Association for Computational Linguistics.

Thibault Sellam, Dipanjan Das, and Ankur Parikh. 2020. BLEURT: Learning robust metrics for text generation. In *Proceedings of the 58th Annual Meeting of the Association for Computational Linguistics*, pages 7881–7892, Online. Association for Computational Linguistics.

Kaitao Song, Xu Tan, Tao Qin, Jianfeng Lu, and Tie-Yan Liu. 2020. Mpnet: Masked and permuted pre-training for language understanding.

Lucia Specia, Frédéric Blain, Marina Fomicheva, Erick Fonseca, Vishrav Chaudhary, Francisco Guzmán, and André F. T. Martins. 2020. Findings of the WMT 2020 shared task on quality estimation. In *Proceedings of the Fifth Conference on Machine Translation*, pages 743–764, Online. Association for Computational Linguistics.

Lucia Specia, Frédéric Blain, Varvara Logacheva, Ramón F. Astudillo, and André F. T. Martins. 2018. Findings of the WMT 2018 shared task on quality estimation. In *Proceedings of the Third Conference on Machine Translation: Shared Task Papers*, pages 689–709, Belgium, Brussels. Association for Computational Linguistics.

Huan Sun, Hao Ma, Xiaodong He, Wen-tau Yih, Yu Su, and Xifeng Yan. 2016. Table cell search for question answering. In *Proceedings of the 25th International Conference on World Wide Web*, pages 771–782.

Yuqing Tang, Chau Tran, Xian Li, Peng-Jen Chen, Naman Goyal, Vishrav Chaudhary, Jiatao Gu, and Angela Fan. 2020. Multilingual translation with extensible multilingual pretraining and finetuning.

Chau Tran, Shruti Bhosale, James Cross, Philipp Koehn, Sergey Edunov, and Angela Fan. 2021. Facebook AI's WMT21 news translation task submission. In *Proceedings of the Sixth Conference on Machine Translation*, pages 205–215, Online. Association for Computational Linguistics.

Alex Wang, Jan Hula, Patrick Xia, Raghavendra Pappagari, R. Thomas McCoy, Roma Patel, Najoung Kim, Ian Tenney, Yinghui Huang, Katherin Yu, Shuning Jin, Berlin Chen, Benjamin Van Durme, Edouard Grave, Ellie Pavlick, and Samuel R. Bowman. 2019. Can you tell me how to get past sesame street? sentence-level pretraining beyond language modeling. In *Proceedings of the 57th Annual Meeting of the Association for Computational Linguistics*, pages 4465–4476, Florence, Italy. Association for Computational Linguistics.

Jianshu Chen Yunkai Zhang Hong Wang Shiyang Li Xiyou Zhou Wenhu Chen, Hongmin Wang and William Yang Wang. 2020. Tabfact : A large-scale dataset for table-based fact verification. In *International Conference on Learning Representations (ICLR)*, Addis Ababa, Ethiopia.

Adina Williams, Nikita Nangia, and Samuel Bowman. 2018. A Broad-Coverage Challenge Corpus for Sentence Understanding through Inference. In *Proceedings of the 2018 Conference of the North American Chapter of the Association for Computational Linguistics: Human Language Technologies*.

Linting Xue, Noah Constant, Adam Roberts, Mihir Kale, Rami Al-Rfou, Aditya Siddhant, Aditya Barua, and Colin Raffel. 2021. mT5: A massively multilingual pre-trained text-to-text transformer. In *Proceedings* of the 2021 Conference of the North American Chapter of the Association for Computational Linguistics: Human Language Technologies*, pages 483–498, Online. Association for Computational Linguistics.

Yinfei Yang, Yuan Zhang, Chris Tar, and Jason Baldridge. 2019. PAWS-X: A cross-lingual adversarial dataset for paraphrase identification. In *Proceedings of the 2019 Conference on Empirical Methods in Natural Language Processing and the 9th International Joint Conference on Natural Language Processing (EMNLP-IJCNLP)*, pages 3687–3692, Hong Kong, China. Association for Computational Linguistics.

Pengcheng Yin, Graham Neubig, Wen-tau Yih, and Sebastian Riedel. 2020. TaBERT: Pretraining for joint understanding of textual and tabular data. In *Proceedings of the 58th Annual Meeting of the Association for Computational Linguistics*, pages 8413–8426, Online. Association for Computational Linguistics.

Ori Yoran, Alon Talmor, and Jonathan Berant. 2021. Turning tables: Generating examples from semi-structured tables for endowing language models with reasoning skills. *arXiv preprint arXiv:2107.07261*.

Tao Yu, Chien-Sheng Wu, Xi Victoria Lin, Bailin Wang, Yi Chern Tan, Xinyi Yang, Dragomir Radev, Richard Socher, and Caiming Xiong. 2021. Grappa: Grammar-augmented pre-training for table semantic parsing. *International Conference of Learning Representation*.

Tao Yu, Rui Zhang, Kai Yang, Michihiro Yasunaga, Dongxu Wang, Zifan Li, James Ma, Irene Li, Qingning Yao, Shanelle Roman, Zilin Zhang, and Dragomir Radev. 2018. Spider: A large-scale human-labeled dataset for complex and cross-domain semantic parsing and text-to-SQL task. In *Proceedings of the 2018 Conference on Empirical Methods in Natural Language Processing*, pages 3911–3921, Brussels, Belgium. Association for Computational Linguistics.

Vicky Zayats, Kristina Toutanova, and Mari Ostendorf. 2021. Representations for question answering from documents with tables and text. In *Proceedings of the 16th Conference of the European Chapter of the Association for Computational Linguistics: Main Volume*, pages 2895–2906, Online. Association for Computational Linguistics.

Hongzhi Zhang, Yingyao Wang, Sirui Wang, Xuezhi Cao, Fuzheng Zhang, and Zhongyuan Wang. 2020. Table fact verification with structure-aware transformer. In *Proceedings of the 2020 Conference on Empirical Methods in Natural Language Processing (EMNLP)*, pages 1624–1629, Online. Association for Computational Linguistics.

Shuo Zhang and Krisztian Balog. 2019. Auto-completion for data cells in relational tables. In *Proceedings of the 28th ACM International Conference on Information and Knowledge Management*, CIKM '19, pages 761–770, New York, NY, USA. ACM.

Tianyi Zhang, Varsha Kishore, Felix Wu, Kilian Q Weinberger, and Yoav Artzi. 2019. BERTScore: Evaluating text generation with BERT. In *International Conference on Learning Representations*.

A Human Annotation Guidelines

Annotators Details. We employed five undergraduate students proficient in English as human evaluation annotators. They were presented with an instruction set with sample examples and annotations before the actual work. We paid the equivalent of 10 cents for every labeled example. The study's authors reviewed random annotations to confirm their quality.

Annotation Guidelines. We refer to the work by (Koehn and Monz, 2006) while setting up our annotation task and instruction guidelines. We gathered 500 table-sentence pairs representing original (en) and back-translated (en) texts per model-language into several Google spreadsheets. We had a total of 108 sheets (4 models, 9 languages, 3 Modes (table-keys, table-values, and hypothesis) and hence 54000 annotation instances. Each sheet was assigned to a single annotator, who was required to adhere to the semantic similarity task requirements, which are outlined below:

1. The Semantic Similarity task requires the annotator to classify each sentence-pair as conveying the same meaning (label 1) or conveying different meaning (label 0) than each other.

2. In case their exists a difference of syntax including spelling mistakes, punctuation error or missing special characters, the annotators was asked to ignore these as long as the sentence meaning is understandable (label 1). In case proper nouns were misspelled, the annotator must judge the spellings as phonetically similar (label 1) or not (otherwise label 0).

3. The annotators were asked to be lenient on the grammar, allowing for active-passive changes and tense change, if the sentences convey close to the same meaning i.e. (label 1).

4. In case acronyms or abbreviations were present in the sentences, the annotators were asked to mark them as same (label 1) if the sentences had proper expansion/contractions.

Code	Language	Language Family	Script Type	# of Speakers
en	English	Germanic	Latin	1.452 Billion
de	German	Germanic	Latin	134.6 Million
fr	French	Romance	Latin	274.1 Million
es	Spanish	Romance	Latin	548.3 Million
af	Afrikaans	Germanic	Latin	17.5 Million
ru	Russian	Balto-Slavik	Cryllic	258.2 Million
zh	Chinese	Sinitic	Hanzi	1.118 Billion
ko	Korean	Koreanic	Hangul	81.7 Million
hi	Hindi	Indo-Aryan	North-Indic	602.2 Million
ar	Arabic	Semitic	Arabic	274.0 Million

Table 5: Details regarding languages provided in the XINFOTABS, from English to Arabic in order of open-source translation resources, refer to OPUS

Train/Test Strategy	Model	en	de	fr	es	af	ru	zh	ko	hi	ar	Model. Avg
English Translated Test (§5.1)	mBERT$_{BASE}$	-	54	53	52	54	52	52	53	52	50	53
	XLM-R$_{LARGE}$ (XNLI)	-	67	66	64	65	65	63	63	63	58	64
	Lang. Avg.	-	60	60	58	60	59	58	58	58	54	**59**
Language Specific Training (§5.2)	mBERT$_{BASE}$	54	54	52	53	50	52	52	51	50	48	52
	XLM-R$_{LARGE}$ (XNLI)	68	66	64	66	63	64	64	64	62	57	64
	Lang. Avg.	61	60	58	60	57	58	58	58	56	53	58
Multiple Language Finetuning Using Only English (§5.3A)	mBERT$_{BASE}$	-	53	54	51	53	53	53	52	51	50	52
	XLM-R$_{LARGE}$ (XNLI)	-	66	67	66	66	65	65	65	64	61	65
	Lang. Avg.	-	59	60	58	59	59	59	59	58	55	**59**
Multiple Language Finetuning Unified Model (§5.3B)	mBERT$_{BASE}$	53	51	53	53	52	51	53	50	50	49	52
	XLM-R$_{LARGE}$ (XNLI)	66	64	64	63	64	64	64	63	63	60	64
	Lang. Avg.	60	58	59	58	58	58	58	56	57	54	58
English Premise Multilingual Hypothesis (§5.4)	mBERT$_{BASE}$	-	49	53	53	51	49	49	50	47	50	50
	XLM-R$_{LARGE}$ (XNLI)	-	63	65	65	64	65	65	63	63	61	64
	Lang. Avg.	-	56	59	59	57	57	57	57	55	55	57

Table 6: Accuracy for baseline tasks on the α_2 set. **Purple** signifies the best task average accuracy, Orange signifies the best language average accuracy, Cerulean signifies the best model accuracy. XLM-R$_{LARGE}$ represent XLM-RoBERTa$_{LARGE}$ model.

Train/Test Strategy	Model	en	de	fr	es	af	ru	zh	ko	hi	ar	Model. Avg.
English Translated Test (§5.1)	mBERT$_{BASE}$	-	52	53	52	53	53	52	52	52	50	52
	XLM-R$_{LARGE}$ (XNLI)	-	65	65	64	63	64	62	62	61	57	63
	Lang avg	-	58	59	58	58	59	57	57	57	53	**58**
Language Specific Training (§5.2)	mBERT$_{BASE}$	52	50	52	53	50	50	51	48	49	49	50
	XLM-R$_{LARGE}$ (XNLI)	67	65	62	64	62	62	63	60	62	57	62
	Lang avg	60	58	57	58	56	56	57	54	56	53	56
Multiple Language Finetuning Using Only English (§5.3A)	mBERT$_{BASE}$	-	52	50	52	52	51	51	49	49	48	50
	XLM-R$_{LARGE}$ (XNLI)	-	65	64	65	62	64	60	63	62	63	63
	Lang avg	-	59	57	58	57	57	56	56	56	54	57
Multiple Language Finetuning Unified Model (§5.3B)	mBERT$_{BASE}$	53	50	51	53	50	50	51	47	50	49	50
	XLM-R$_{LARGE}$ (XNLI)	66	64	64	64	63	64	63	62	63	60	63
	Lang avg	60	57	57	58	56	57	57	55	56	54	57
English Premise Multilingual Hypothesis (§5.4)	mBERT$_{BASE}$	-	51	50	51	50	50	47	45	48	48	49
	XLM-R$_{LARGE}$ (XNLI)	-	63	63	64	62	62	62	60	61	60	62
	Lang avg	-	57	57	57	56	56	55	54	55	54	56

Table 7: Accuracy for baseline tasks on the α_3 set. **Purple** signifies the best task average accuracy, Orange signifies the best language average accuracy, Cerulean signifies the best model accuracy. XLM-R$_{LARGE}$ represent XLM-RoBERTa$_{LARGE}$ model.

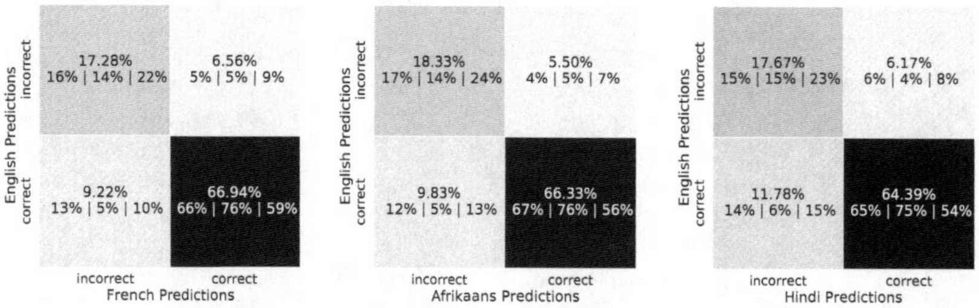

(a) (b) (c)

Figure 2: Predictions of XLM-RoBERTa for English vs (a) French, (b) Afrikaans, (c) Hindi. The percentage on top in each block represents the average across all three labels with each label percentage given below it in the order of ENTAILMENT, NEUTRAL and CONTRADICTION. (cf. Appendix §E)

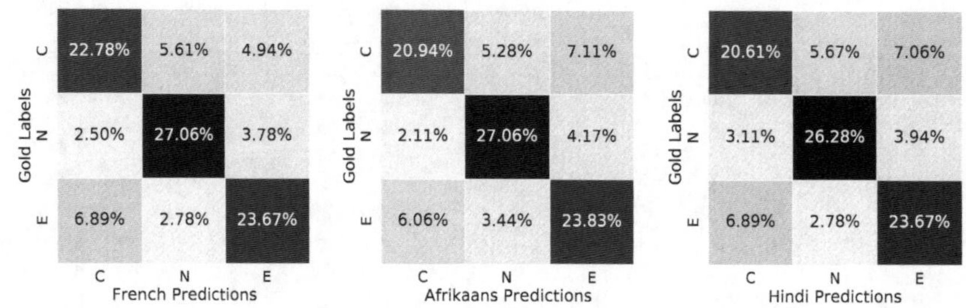

(a) (b) (c)

Figure 3: Confusion Matrix: Gold Labels vs predictions of XLM-R for (a) French, (b) Afrikaans, (c) Hindi

Categories	ENTAILMENT					NEUTRAL					CONTRADICTION				
	En	Fr	Af	Hi	Avg.	En	Fr	Af	Hi	Avg.	En	Fr	Af	Hi	Avg.
Person	79	71	75	73	74	82	81	78	81	81	59	67	54	56	59
Musician	**88**	77	78	76	80	87	87	91	82	87	70	69	60	69	67
Movie	70	63	57	63	63	85	93	85	87	88	**81**	**76**	**78**	65	**75**
Album	76	76	81	62	74	**95**	90	86	**90**	**90**	76	**76**	67	62	70
City	73	58	60	67	65	71	69	65	63	67	67	54	50	52	56
Country	74	61	65	63	66	74	70	76	76	74	74	72	76	69	73
Painting	83	79	75	67	76	83	**96**	**92**	83	89	71	71	71	71	71
Animal	79	75	79	79	78	75	58	83	67	71	71	75	67	58	68
Food&Drink	**88**	83	75	**88**	**83**	83	79	71	79	78	67	63	58	54	60
Organization	83	**100**	**83**	50	79	67	67	67	67	67	67	67	67	**83**	71
Other	75	73	67	73	72	73	84	84	75	79	76	68	71	62	69
Avg.	79	74	72	69	74	80	79	80	77	79	71	69	65	64	67

Table 8: Category wise accuracy scores of XLM-R (large) for four languages: namely English (En), French (Fr), Afrikaans (Af) and Hindi (Hi). Orange denotes the least score in the column and **Purple** denotes the highest score in the column.

Reasoning type	ENTAILMENT					NEUTRAL					CONTRADICTION				
	H.En	En	Fr	Af	Ko	H.En	En	Fr	Af	Ko	H.En	En	Fr	Af	Ko
Coref	8	6	6	6	4	22	19	19	20	19	13	10	9	7	8
Entity Type	6	5	5	5	5	8	6	6	6	6	6	6	6	4	5
KCS	31	21	19	17	22	21	20	17	19	18	24	18	17	17	20
Lexical Reasoning	5	4	4	4	3	3	2	2	2	1	4	1	1	1	1
Multirow	20	14	11	11	11	16	13	12	13	11	17	15	14	10	13
Named Entity	2	0	0	0	1	2	1	1	1	2	1	1	1	1	1
Negation	0	0	0	0	0	0	0	0	0	0	6	5	5	4	5
Numerical	11	10	7	8	8	3	3	2	3	2	7	5	6	4	4
Quantification	4	2	2	2	2	13	10	10	12	10	6	2	1	2	3
Simple Lookup	3	2	1	2	2	0	0	0	0	0	1	0	1	0	0
Subjective/OOT	6	3	4	4	3	41	37	35	36	37	6	3	4	2	3
Temporal	19	16	12	13	14	11	6	6	6	5	25	18	20	15	19

Table 9: Reasoning wise number of correct predictions of XLM-R (large) for four languages: namely English (En), French (Fr), Afrikaans (Af) and Hindi (Hi) along with human scores for the english dataset

5. In presence of numbers or dates, the annotators were asked to be extremely strict and label even slightly differing dates or numbers like (XXXI v.s. 30) as completely different (label 0).
6. In case of any further ambiguity, the judgement was left to the annotators human far-sight as long as the adhere to the task definition.

We estimated the accuracy of human verification for every models and languages by averaging the annotator labels.

B Multilingual Models Hyperparameters

The XLM-R_{LARGE} (XNLI) model was taken from HuggingFace[9] models and finetuned using PyTorch Framework[10] on Google Colaboratory[11] which offer a single P100 GPU. We utilized accuracy as our metric of choice, same as INFOTABS. We used Adagrad (Li and Orabona, 2019) as our optimizer with a learning rate of $1 * 10^{-4}$. We ran our finetuning script for ten epochs with a validation interval of 1 epoch, and early stopping callback enabled with the patience of 2. Given the large model size, we had to use a batch size of 4.

The $mBERT_{BASE}$ (cased) model was trained on TPUv2 8 cores using the PyTorch Lightning[12] Framework. AdamW (Loshchilov and Hutter, 2017) was our choice of optimizer with learning rate $5 * 10^{-6}$. We ran our finetuning script for ten epochs with a validation interval of 0.5 epochs, and early stopping callback enabled with the patience of 3. Given the model's small size, we used a batch size of 64 (8 per TPU core).

C Adversarial Sets (α_2 and α_3) Performance

Tables 6 and 7 show the results for all baseline tasks on the Adversarial Validation Sets α_2 and α_3.

D Evaluating Cross-Lingual Transfer

We are also interested in knowing whether training in one language can help transfer knowledge across other languages or not. We answer the question: *What are models of cross-lingual transfer performance?*. Since we have separate models trained on languages from our dataset available, we tested them on all other languages other than the training language to study cross-lingual transfer.

The TrLangAvg scores (Training Language Average) from 10 show how models trained on XINFOTABS for one language perform on other languages for α_1, α_2 and α_3 sets respectively. XLM-R (XNLI) outperforms mBERT across all tasks. English has the best cross-lingual transferability on mBERT, whereas Spanish has the best cross-lingual transferability on XLM-R(XNLI) for the α_1 set. On mBERT, German has the best cross-lingual transferability for the α_2 dataset. On XLM-R (XNLI), German and Spanish have the best cross-lingual transferability. On mBERT, English has the best cross-lingual transferability for the α_3 dataset. On XLM-R (XNLI), English and Spanish have the best cross-lingual transferability. Furthermore, the EvLangAvg score (Evaluation Language Average) score was comparable for all languages except approximately 4% lower for Arabic ('ar') language with XLM-R(XNLI) model on all three test sets.

Overall, we observe that finetuning models on high resource languages improve their cross-lingual transfer capacity considerably more than finetuning models on low resource languages.

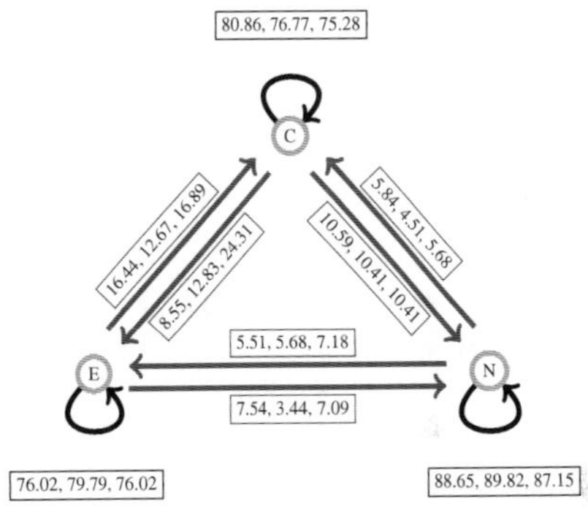

Figure 4: Consistency graph for XLM-R (large) predictions of English vs (a) French (b) Afrikaans (c) Hindi in that order respectively.

E Robustness and Consistency

In this part, we examine the findings for several languages and delve a little more into the key disparities in performance across them. We compare the results of the experiments for §5.2 setting for α_1 set of best-performing language (en) with three languages - (a) A high resource language (fr), (b) A mid resource language (af) and c) A low resource language (hi). We compute four numbers for each of the languages (l) (where l is (fr), (af), or (hi)) and (en) - the proportion of instances when (a) both are right, (b) both are erroneous (c) correct (en) but incorrect (l), and

[9] huggingface.co [10] pytorch.org [11] Google Colaboratory
[12] PyTorch Lightning

(d) correct (l) but incorrect (en). We compute this number overall as well independently for each of the inference labels, as shown in Figure 2.

We note that the majority of instances were correctly categorized in both English and all three other languages. This is followed by the number of instances in which English and all other languages categorised examples inaccurately. Additionally, we notice a greater proportion of samples that are correctly identified by English but wrongly classified by all other languages, as opposed to the contrary. Furthermore, the label NEUTRAL has the highest proportion of correctly classified examples across all languages, whereas the label CONTRADICTION has the lowest.

In Figure 3, we notice that the CONTRADICTION gets confused a lot with ENTAILMENT label across all the languages. The difference between the accuracy for the CONTRADICTION label of French vs Afrikaans and Hindi can entirely be attributed to this sort of confusion. Furthermore, ENTAILMENT gets quite confused with CONTRADICTION.

In Figure 4, we see the greatest language inconsistency with ENTAILMENT label going towards CONTRADICTION across all the languages, though this inconsistency is least in Afrikaans. The inconsistency for CONTRADICTION label being predicted as ENTAILMENT is increasing across resource size of languages from French having the least to Hindi having the highest. Otherwise, the inconsistency across languages is rather low, showing that the XLM-R_{LARGE} model is quite consistent across languages.

In Table 8, we can observe that our model on average performs worst for all ENTAILMENT belonging to Movie category, NEUTRAL and CONTRADICTION belonging to City category. In general, our model performs the worst for all hypothesis belonging to the City category possibly because of the involvement of larger table sizes on average and highly numeric and specific hypothesis statements as compared to the rest of the categories. Our models perform extremely well on all ENTAILMENT in FoodDrink category because of their smaller table size on average and hypothesis requiring no external knowledge to confirm as compared to CONTRADICTION. For ENTAILMENT our model performs remarkably well on Organization category for French, getting all the hypothesis labels correct. While for NEUTRAL, it performs well for Paintings in French language. Lastly, it performs marginally well for CONTRADICTION on Hindi for Organization as compared to the highest performing category for CONTRADICTION in English i.e. the Movie category. All language averages perform in the order of their language resource which is expected from Table 4.

Table 9 depicts a subset of the validation set which has been labeled based on different reasoning mechanisms that the model must employ to categorize the hypothesis correctly. We found the reasoning accuracy scores for 4 languages along with human evaluation score for comparison. Upon observation, we can see that regardless of language, human scores are better than the model we utilize. The variation in language is mostly minimal, but on average our model performs best for English. We notice that for some reasoning types, like Negation and Simple Look-up, humans and the model get no hypothesis right, showing the toughness of the problem. For Numerical based reasoning as well as Coref type reasoning, our model comes very close to human score evaluation. However, overall we are still far from human level performance at TNLI and much scope remains to betterment of models on this task.

Test-Split	Model	TrLang	en	de	fr	es	af	ru	zh	ar	ko	hi	TrLangAvg
α_1	mBERT$_{\text{BASE}}$	en	67	64	63	62	61	61	60	56	58	58	61
		de	63	65	61	62	60	59	57	56	56	57	60
		fr	64	62	65	62	61	59	59	55	53	57	60
		es	62	62	**63**	63	61	60	60	57	57	58	60
		af	**62**	61	61	60	62	59	57	55	55	55	59
		ru	63	61	61	60	59	64	59	56	55	55	59
		zh	55	56	58	56	59	57	63	55	57	58	57
		ar	57	**58**	**58**	57	**58**	**58**	57	57	53	57	57
		ko	58	59	58	57	57	56	58	55	61	57	58
		hi	59	58	59	58	57	58	58	56	54	63	58
	EvLangAvg		**61**	**61**	**61**	60	60	59	59	56	56	58	59
	XLM-R (XNLI)	en	76	73	71	73	71	71	71	63	70	69	71
		de	74	75	74	72	71	70	69	63	71	68	71
		fr	73	**74**	74	72	72	70	71	64	70	70	71
		es	**74**	73	74	74	72	71	72	65	71	69	72
		af	**72**	**72**	71	71	72	70	70	63	70	68	70
		ru	**73**	**73**	72	71	71	71	71	64	70	67	70
		zh	72	72	70	71	70	69	73	64	70	69	70
		ar	**71**	**71**	70	70	69	70	**71**	68	70	68	70
		ko	**72**	71	**72**	71	70	69	71	64	71	69	70
		hi	**73**	**73**	71	72	70	70	70	64	69	71	70
	EvLangAvg		**73**	**73**	72	72	71	70	71	64	70	69	70
α_2	mBERT$_{\text{BASE}}$	en	54	53	53	53	51	52	50	49	50	47	51
		de	54	54	53	53	52	52	50	49	50	48	52
		fr	52	51	52	53	50	50	48	49	51	47	50
		es	52	50	50	53	47	51	48	49	46	46	49
		af	49	**50**	**50**	49	**50**	**50**	47	48	48	46	49
		ru	51	50	51	51	51	52	49	49	49	49	50
		zh	49	48	49	48	49	49	52	47	48	48	49
		ar	**49**	48	**49**	48	47	48	47	48	47	47	48
		ko	49	49	50	48	48	47	50	47	51	49	49
		hi	48	47	47	48	48	49	48	46	48	50	48
	EvLangAvg		**51**	50	50	50	49	50	49	48	49	48	50
	XLM-R (XNLI)	en	68	65	64	64	64	63	62	58	63	59	63
		de	**67**	66	66	65	64	63	62	57	64	61	64
		fr	**67**	64	64	65	62	60	60	58	62	60	62
		es	**67**	66	65	66	63	64	62	57	64	61	64
		af	**66**	64	64	64	63	62	63	57	62	59	62
		ru	**66**	64	64	63	62	64	62	57	61	60	62
		zh	**67**	65	65	64	63	64	64	58	64	61	62
		ar	**64**	61	62	61	60	60	60	57	60	58	60
		ko	**65**	63	63	63	61	62	62	57	64	59	62
		hi	**67**	64	65	65	63	64	62	58	60	62	63
	EvLangAvg		**66**	64	64	64	63	63	62	57	62	60	63
α_3	mBERT$_{\text{BASE}}$	en	52	52	51	53	49	50	49	47	46	47	50
		de	50	50	**51**	50	51	48	48	44	46	48	49
		fr	52	52	52	53	50	50	49	46	44	47	50
		es	50	50	51	53	48	48	46	46	46	46	50
		af	50	50	50	51	50	49	47	47	45	48	49
		ru	**50**	48	49	**50**	49	50	47	45	45	46	48
		zh	49	49	50	50	49	50	51	46	48	49	49
		ar	**49**	**49**	**49**	**49**	48	**49**	48	49	47	48	48
		ko	47	46	47	47	44	45	45	43	48	**48**	46
		hi	**50**	49	49	49	48	46	48	46	47	50	48
	EvLangAvg		**50**	49	**50**	**50**	49	48	48	46	46	48	49
	XLM-R (XNLI)	en	67	65	61	64	62	64	63	58	65	62	63
		de	**65**	65	63	61	63	63	61	56	61	60	62
		fr	**66**	64	62	63	62	61	61	56	60	62	62
		es	**66**	65	63	64	63	63	62	59	61	62	63
		af	**65**	64	61	62	62	60	61	56	60	59	61
		ru	**65**	63	61	62	62	62	61	56	60	62	61
		zh	**65**	64	62	63	62	62	63	57	62	60	62
		ar	**63**	62	62	61	61	60	60	57	60	60	61
		ko	**64**	62	61	62	60	63	61	56	60	62	61
		hi	**64**	63	62	63	61	61	60	58	60	62	61
	EvLangAvg		**65**	64	62	63	62	62	61	57	61	61	62

Table 10: Evaluation of cross lingual transfer abilities of models on α_1, α_2, and α_3 evaluation set. TrLang refers to the language the model has been finetuned on and EvLang refers to the language the model has been evaluated on. **Purple**, Orange and Cerulean represent the highest score in the row, column and both together respectively.

Neural Machine Translation for Fact-checking Temporal Claims

Marco Mori[1], Paolo Papotti[2], Luigi Bellomarini[1], and Oliver Giudice[1]

[1]Bank of Italy, Italy
[2]EURECOM, France

Abstract

Computational fact-checking aims at supporting the verification process of textual claims by exploiting trustworthy sources. However, there are large classes of complex claims that cannot be automatically verified, for instance those related to temporal reasoning. To this aim, in this work, we focus on the verification of economic claims against time series sources. Starting from given textual claims in natural language, we propose a neural machine translation approach to produce respective queries expressed in a recently proposed temporal fragment of the Datalog language. The adopted deep neural approach shows promising preliminary results for the translation of 10 categories of claims extracted from real use cases.

1 Introduction

False and misleading information spreading on media negatively impacts our society by affecting people opinions and behaviours. To oppose such phenomena, *fact-checking* is the process aiming at verifying the correctness of facts in a piece of text, i.e., *claims* (Nakov et al., 2021). To this end, claims have to be debunked against trustworthy structured and non-structured sources. In this work, we report on our effort on statistical claims in collaboration with a national central bank in Europe. Specifically, we focus on claims about economic events and trends that should be checked against temporal data sequences, namely *time series*, the standard format for time-based data in this domain.

Fact-checking organizations debunk such claims applying a typically manual process to extract claims from text, retrieving pieces of evidence from relevant sources, and finally, reaching a verdict using such evidence. Given the large amount of information produced and shared online, this process cannot guarantee that an adequate number of economic claims is debunked. To enable scalability, statistical claims could be automatically verified

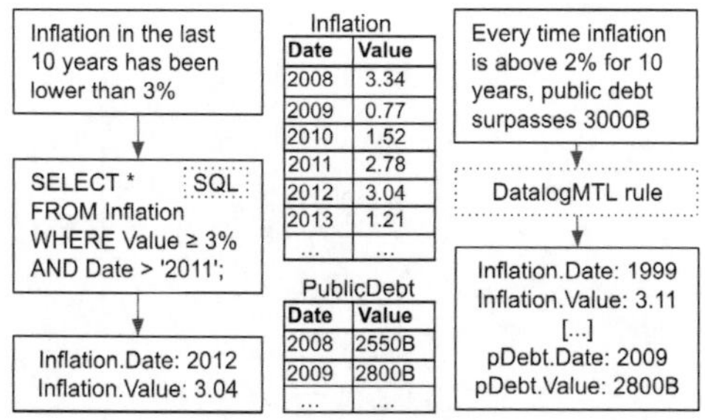

Figure 1: Examples of a claim verified with a SQL query (left) and a complex claim tested with a Datalog rule (right). In both cases, the result is not empty, thus the claim is false based on the evidence in the time series.

to support checkers in their work. In order to be interpretable to the human, not only should the automatic verification provide a label for the given claim, but also a clear explanation of the adopted reasoning process as well as the evidence used to draw the conclusion.

Declarative languages offer a valid solution to both challenges. Mature data modeling languages balance computational complexity and expressive power, addressing the scalability challenges. Interpretability is a major advantage of declarative languages, with well-known semantics applied to the ground data in a deductive, top-down approach (Hansen and Rieger, 2019).

Different solutions translate text formats to executable high-level languages, e.g., SQL queries, typically through neural architectures (Katsogiannis-Meimarakis and Koutrika, 2021; Saeed and Papotti, 2021). While these approaches exhibit promising results, they do not effectively translate claims including temporal aspects into an executable form. This depends on their limited capability in capturing the temporal logic of claims.

Example. Consider a central bank that offers a service to fact-check economic claims. Reference information is available in the standard format of time-series. The bank has data about economic

Proceedings of the Fifth Fact Extraction and VERification Workshop (FEVER), pages 78 - 82
May 26, 2022

measures, such as inflation, public debt, employment rate, interest rates, and about events such as economic crises, and salary increments. The example in Figure 1 shows the inflation and public debt metrics with key-value tables.

While some claims can be easily written as SQL queries for their verification, for most of them this is very difficult, or unfeasible in some cases. Consider the claims *(i)* "Inflation in the last 10 years has been lower than 3%" and *(ii)* "Every time inflation is above 2% for 10 years, public debt surpasses 3000B". A possible SQL query to verify claim *(i)* through counter-example detection is reported in the left-hand side of Figure 1. For Claim *(ii)*, a script should evaluate, for each year in the dataset, the value of public debt and then check a condition over inflation for the previous 10 years. Although such expression can be written in SQL for one given year, our claim requires checking the condition for every possible year, which turns out to be unfeasible or extremely laborious and inefficient in SQL. With DatalogMTL (Brandt et al., 2018), a Datalog fragment that incorporates temporal operators, we can represent our expression as:

$$\bot := \boxminus_{[0,10]}\ \mathit{inflationGt}(y), y = 0.02, \mathit{public\_debt}(x), x \leq 3000B$$

The rule intercepts the cases in which Claim *(ii)* is violated. In fact, it is triggered whenever the body (right-hand side) is satisfied, meaning that the inflation is found greater than 2% for the 10 preceding years but the public debt is below or equal to 3000B. Specifically, the logical premise of our claim ("Every time inflation is above 2%") is checked through the temporal operator $\boxminus_\varrho$, i.e., "*always true in the interval* $\varrho = [t - 10y, t]$", so that for the rule to be triggered at a point in time t, the logical conclusion of our claim must be false, i.e., $\mathit{public\_debt}(x), x \leq 3000B$. The evaluation of the rule checks the claim and produces human-understandable counter-examples (Figure 1).

In this paper, we propose a neural machine translation approach to fact-check numerical temporal claims. In particular, our approach synthesizes temporal data queries (rules) from input claims for the verification of temporal claims. While there have been efforts to use neural architectures for generating SQL scripts (Yin et al., 2021), to the best of our knowledge, there is no support to translate textual claims into Datalog rules (Brandt et al., 2018).

The main contributions of our approach are: *(i)* the adoption of DatalogMTL to encode as rules a large class of temporal economic claims thus capturing their temporal logic, *(ii)* the rule synthesis according to our proposed *fine-tuned neural T5 model* (Raffel et al., 2020).

Our model is generated based on a dataset of manually crafted claim-query pairs inspired by economic newspapers and the Federal Reserve dataset (Fred, 2022). Finally, a validation phase attests the ability of our model to automatically synthesize newly generated claims unseen during fine-tuning.

2 Language and Templates

In this section we present the DatalogMTL formalism, the reference data model, and a categorization of claim-query pairs based on their semantics.

Temporal Datalog. We adopt *Datalog Metric Temporal Logic (DatalogMTL)*, a temporal logic-based language that has recently received great attention from the AI and database communities (Walega et al., 2019, 2020, 2021). DatalogMTL extends Datalog with metric temporal logic operators over the rational timeline. We consider DatalogMTL rules of the form $\bot := A_1, \ldots, A_k$, for $k \geq 0$, where all A_i are literals that follow the grammar $A ::= \top \mid \bot \mid P(\boldsymbol{\tau}) \mid \boxminus_\varrho A \mid \diamondminus_\varrho A$, with ϱ being a *non-negative* interval, and P an atom (on a predicate having either functional or infix notation) over a tuple of terms (i.e., variables and constants) $\boldsymbol{\tau}$. The conjunction of A is the rule *body* and commas denote the logical and ($\wedge$).

Given a database D, the semantics of a DatalogMTL rule is defined through interpretations. An interpretation $\mathfrak{M}$ specifies for each time point t, whether a ground atom $P(\mathbf{a})$ from D is true at t, in which case we write $\mathfrak{M}, t \models P(\mathbf{a})@t$. The @ symbol denotes the time reference for an atom.

An interpretation that satisfies all atoms of the body triggers the rule. The box minus $\boxminus_\varrho$ operator checks if a ground atom is *continuously* true in the interval ϱ, that is, $\mathfrak{M}, t \models \boxminus_\varrho A$ iff $\mathfrak{M}, s \models A$ for all s, with $t - s \in \varrho$. The diamond minus $\diamondminus_\varrho$ operator checks if a ground atom is true at least once in the interval ϱ, that is, $\mathfrak{M}, t \models \diamondminus_\varrho A$ iff $\mathfrak{M}, s \models A$ for some s, with $t - s \in \varrho$.

Data Model. We rely on existing data sources containing time series, each representing an economic metric and following the *key-value* format, where *key* represents a time instant and *value* the corresponding measure. Time series with multiple attributes can also be treated after a pre-processing phase which restructures them into multiple tables having replicated key values. Instances of our data model straightforwardly derive from widely adopted on-line economic libraries such as the Federal Reserve Economic Data (FRED) and the datasource exposed by the central bank in our project.

Query templates. We distinguish temporal claims according to their semantics and organize them into templates, providing for each of them the corresponding DatalogMTL rule. Our rules can be efficiently executed on a DatalogMTL engine (Bellomarini et al., 2021; Benedikt et al., 2017).

In Table 1, we collect 10 different templates along with a claim/rule example in our scenario. It is not our intention to produce an exhaustive list of all the admissible templates, instead we aim at showing the feasibility of generating the correct rules for claims falling into any of the given input set of templates. Among others, the rule for Template 2 is triggered if the inflation during 2011 surpassed 2%. Our claims do not specify the country, as we refer to one single national central bank.

3 Translating Claims to DatalogMTL

In the context of Neural Machine Translation (Sutskever et al., 2014; Bahdanau et al., 2015) pre-trained Language Models (PLMs) neural networks based on Transformers excel at handling Natural Language (NL) sequences in understanding and generation tasks (Vaswani et al., 2017; Devlin et al., 2019). These models are typically pre-trained on large text corpora in an unsupervised manner, for example by predicting the missing tokens in each sentence. Many Natural Language Processing (NLP) tasks can benefit from the NL understanding and generation capabilities of PLMs by means of *fine-tuning* with task-specific data through transfer learning. Fine-tuning is performed in a supervised manner, by providing the labelled input.

Our approach fine-tunes the T5 model to use its text-to-text capabilities for our text-to-rule translation task. To this end, we generate and augment a fine-tuning set of textual input (claims) and output (rules) labels to specialize the T5 model.

Starting from a template-based categorization of the rules (Table 1), we transform each pair ($\langle$claim *NL*, rule *DL*$\rangle$) into a full-text specification: *NL* is prefixed by *"datalog translation:"*, which identifies the downstream translation task; for *DL* we safely remove the symbol $\perp$ appearing in all queries (thus non necessary to predict) and replace math symbols with text snippets.

We exploit the set of templates and the time series to augment the fine-tuning dataset. For each claim, we create a set of variants having the same semantics but different syntax. We replace the actual values of economic metrics, events, numeric values, temporal and comparison text snippets with specific placeholders. We show the process for claims belonging to templates 3 (1,2) e 2 (3,4):

```
1: In <instant> <metric> reached the
<max-min> since the last <epoch>.
2: During the last <epoch> <metric> is
<higher-lower> than in <instant>.
3: <metric> during <instant> was
<higher-lower> than <value>.
4: The value of <metric> was
<higher-lower> than <value> in <instant>.
```

We replace their rules with placeholders:

```
1-2: Time op. star[<epoch>] <metric>(y),
<metric>(x)@[<instant>],x <comparator> y
3-4: <metric>(x)@[<instant>],x
<comparator> <value>
```

We then replace the placeholders with the actual input values from our data sources:

```
1: In 2020 inflation reached the maximum
since the last six years.
2: During the last six years inflation
is lower than in 2020.
3: Inflation during 2011 was higher
than 0.02.
4: The value of inflation was higher
than 0.02 in 2011.
```

We apply the same process to the rules:

```
1-2: Time op. star[six years] inflation
(y), inflation(x)@[2020],x less than y
3-4: inflation(x)@[2011],x less than
equal to 0.02
```

4 Training and Validation Results

We describe: *(i)* how we obtained the fine-tuned T5 model and *(ii)* how we used it to automatically translate textual claims into rules. Our results are based on the exact string matches accuracy of predicted DatalogMTL rules against the ground truth. Traditional BLEU and ROUGE metrics are not used here since they may lead to good accuracy also for minimal variations of the predicted rules resulting to drastically different execution outcomes.

Model fine-tuning. Following our translation approach we generated 60K $\langle NL, DL\rangle$ pairs uniformly distributed among the 10 templates after undersampling the most populated classes. After splitting the dataset into training and test sets and setting the architecture parameters, we fine-tune a T5-base

#	Template	Claim / Rule Example
1	Metric at two time instants	In 2020 the inflation was higher than in year 2021 $\bot := \textit{inflation}(x)@[2020], \textit{inflation}(y)@[2021], x \leq y$
2	Metric value at single instant	Inflation during 2011 was higher than 0.02 $\bot := \textit{inflation}(x)@[2011], x \leq 0.02$
3	Metric at single instant w.r.t. previous epoch value	In 2020 inflation reached the maximum since the last six years $\bot := \diamondminus_{[0,6]}\textit{inflation}(y), \textit{inflation}(x)@[2020], x < y$
4	Metric at a given epoch	During the last ten years the inflation has always been higher than 0.02 $\bot := \diamondminus_{[0,10]}\textit{inflation}(x), x \leq 0.02, \textit{true}@[\textit{today}]$
5	Metric at given epoch implies metric at single instant	After ten years of inflation above 2%, public debt surpassed 3000 $\bot := \textit{public debt}(x), x \leq 3000, \boxminus_{[0,10]}\textit{inflationGt}(y), y = 0.02$
6	Event at a single instant	An economic crisis occurred in 2008 $\bot := \textit{economic crisis}(x)@[2008], x = \textit{False}$
7	Event at a given epoch	A salary increment has been observed during the last 3 years $\bot := \boxminus_{[0,3]}\textit{salary increment}(x), x = \textit{False}, \textit{true}@[\textit{today}]$
8	Metric at given epoch implies required event	If inflation for the last ten years was higher than 0.02, we have a salary increment $\bot := \textit{salary increment}(x), x = \textit{False}, \boxminus_{[0,10]}\textit{inflationGt}(z), z = 0.02$
9	Event at given epoch implies metric at a single instant	Till to 5 years after a stock market crash, inflation remained below 0.02 $\bot := \textit{inflation}(x), x \geq 0.02, \diamondminus_{[0,5]}\textit{stock market crash}(\mathrm{z}), z = \textit{True}$
10	Event at epoch and metric at instant imply required event	In the 3 years after a salary increment, if inflation is lower than 0.02, there is a salary increment $\bot := \textit{salary increment}(y), y = \textit{False}, \diamondminus_{[0,3]}\textit{salary increment}(z), z = \textit{True}, \textit{inflation}(x), x < 0.02$

Table 1: Query templates with the respective claim and temporal Datalog example.

model (Google, 2022) to generate our prediction model. This process has been carried out in 3 hours on a NC12s_v2 machine with 12 CPUs, 224GB RAM and a P100 Nvidia GPU.

Model prediction. We apply our fine-tuned model on newly generated input claims in any of our 10 templates. For each claim, we generate a set of variants sharing the same semantics but with different syntax by using 3 paraphrasing tools from the NL-Augmenter Python framework (Goyal and Durrett, 2020; Dopierre et al., 2021; Kumar et al., 2019). We generate 30 variants per claim after replacing placeholder variables with a set of reference values. We then place back placeholders and eliminate duplicated and erroneous claims, i.e., those that have a different set of placeholders w.r.t. the starting claim. Finally, placeholders are replaced with actual values before randomly selecting 5000 claims balanced across template categories. Given such newly generated test set (average Jaccard distance from the training set was 0.317), we predict the DatalogMTL rules with our model. The model correctly predicts (in less than one hour) 4495 over 5000 claims resulting in a 0.90 average accuracy.

Table 2 provides accuracy results about templates, each characterized by 4 features: number of rule placeholders, epoch vs instant-based placeholders, number of comparison operators, and claim type, i.e., a simple statement or a more complex conditional phrase. Results show decreasing prediction performance with claims of higher complexity, corresponding to rules with mixed time placeholders and comparison operators on metrics.

Template	# Plcs	Time	# Ops	Type	Accuracy
1	5	I+I	1	S	0.794
2	4	I	1	S	0.934
3	5	I+E	1	S	0.636
4	4	E	1	S	0.970
5	7	E	2	C	0.802
6	2	I	0	S	0.986
7	2	E	0	S	0.978
8	5	E	1	C	0.974
9	5	E	1	C	0.984
10	6	E	1	C	0.932

Table 2: Prediction accuracy for claims grouped by template. *# Plcs* denotes the # of rule placeholders, *Time* reports instant (*I*) and epoch (*E*) placeholders, *# Ops* is the # of comparison operators on metrics, *Type* denotes conditional (*C*) and simple (*S*) phrases.

5 Conclusion

This work shows that numerical temporal claims can be computationally verified exploiting time series. While preliminary results are promising, one major challenge is the lack of training data for the rule generation module. Templates are an effective solution, but the coverage of the system depends on the number of deployed templates. We are also working on how to create data explanations for true claims, as now we only show counter-examples. One road is to identify examples by perturbing the Datalog rule, as studied for SQL queries (Wu et al., 2017). We are looking at how to improve the validation step by comparing the effects of the generated rules, instead of their syntactical equivalence and by testing a real-world benchmark of claims.

Acknowledgments. We thank Livia Blasi, Markus Nissl, and Mohammed Saeed for their help.

References

Dzmitry Bahdanau, Kyunghyun Cho, and Yoshua Bengio. 2015. Neural machine translation by jointly learning to align and translate. In *3rd International Conference on Learning Representations, ICLR 2015*.

Luigi Bellomarini, Markus Nissl, and Emanuel Sallinger. 2021. Query evaluation in DatalogMTL - taming infinite query results. *CoRR*, abs/2109.10691.

Michael Benedikt, George Konstantinidis, Giansalvatore Mecca, Boris Motik, Paolo Papotti, Donatello Santoro, and Efthymia Tsamoura. 2017. Benchmarking the chase. In *PODS*, pages 37–52. ACM.

Sebastian Brandt, Elem Güzel Kalayci, Vladislav Ryzhikov, Guohui Xiao, and Michael Zakharyaschev. 2018. Querying log data with metric temporal logic. *J. Artif. Intell. Res.*, 62:829–877.

Jacob Devlin, Ming-Wei Chang, Kenton Lee, and Kristina Toutanova. 2019. BERT: Pre-training of deep bidirectional transformers for language understanding. In *Proceedings of the 2019 Conference of the North American Chapter of the Association for Computational Linguistics: Human Language Technologies, Volume 1 (Long and Short Papers)*, pages 4171–4186. Association for Computational Linguistics.

Thomas Dopierre, Christophe Gravier, and Wilfried Logerais. 2021. Protaugment: Unsupervised diverse short-texts paraphrasing for intent detection meta-learning. *CoRR*, abs/2105.12995.

Fred. 2022. FRED - federal reserve economic data. `https://fred.stlouisfed.org/`.

Google. 2022. T5-base model. `https://huggingface.co/t5-base`.

Tanya Goyal and Greg Durrett. 2020. Preordering for controlled paraphrase generation. In *Proceedings of the 58th Annual Meeting of the Association for Computational Linguistics*, pages 238–252, Online. Association for Computational Linguistics.

Lars Kai Hansen and Laura Rieger. 2019. Interpretability in intelligent systems - A new concept? In *Explainable AI*, volume 11700 of *Lecture Notes in Computer Science*, pages 41–49. Springer.

George Katsogiannis-Meimarakis and Georgia Koutrika. 2021. A deep dive into deep learning approaches for text-to-sql systems. In *Proceedings of the 2021 International Conference on Management of Data*, pages 2846–2851.

Ashutosh Kumar, Satwik Bhattamishra, Manik Bhandari, and Partha Talukdar. 2019. Submodular optimization-based diverse paraphrasing and its effectiveness in data augmentation. In *Proceedings of the 2019 Conference of the North American Chapter of the Association for Computational Linguistics: Human Language Technologies, Volume 1 (Long and Short Papers)*, pages 3609–3619. Association for Computational Linguistics.

Preslav Nakov, David P. A. Corney, Maram Hasanain, Firoj Alam, Tamer Elsayed, Alberto Barrón-Cedeño, Paolo Papotti, Shaden Shaar, and Giovanni Da San Martino. 2021. Automated fact-checking for assisting human fact-checkers. In *IJCAI*, pages 4551–4558. ijcai.org.

Colin Raffel, Noam Shazeer, Adam Roberts, Katherine Lee, Sharan Narang, Michael Matena, Yanqi Zhou, Wei Li, and Peter J. Liu. 2020. Exploring the limits of transfer learning with a unified text-to-text transformer. *Journal of Machine Learning Research*, 21(140):1–67.

Mohammed Saeed and Paolo Papotti. 2021. Fact-checking statistical claims with tables. *IEEE Data Eng. Bull.*, 44(3):27–38.

Ilya Sutskever, Oriol Vinyals, and Quoc V Le. 2014. Sequence to sequence learning with neural networks. In *Advances in Neural Information Processing Systems, NIPS 2014*.

Ashish Vaswani, Noam Shazeer, Niki Parmar, Jakob Uszkoreit, Llion Jones, Aidan N Gomez, Łukasz Kaiser, and Illia Polosukhin. 2017. Attention is all you need. *Advances in neural information processing systems*, 30:6000–6010.

Przemyslaw Andrzej Walega, Bernardo Cuenca Grau, Mark Kaminski, and Egor V. Kostylev. 2020. Tractable fragments of datalog with metric temporal operators. In *IJCAI*, pages 1919–1925. ijcai.org.

Przemyslaw Andrzej Walega, Mark Kaminski, and Bernardo Cuenca Grau. 2019. Reasoning over streaming data in metric temporal datalog. In *AAAI*, pages 3092–3099. AAAI Press.

Przemyslaw Andrzej Walega, Michal Zawidzki, and Bernardo Cuenca Grau. 2021. Finitely materialisable datalog programs with metric temporal operators. In *KR*, pages 619–628.

You Wu, Pankaj K. Agarwal, Chengkai Li, Jun Yang, and Cong Yu. 2017. Computational fact checking through query perturbations. *ACM Trans. Database Syst.*, 42(1):4:1–4:41.

Xiaoyu Yin, Dagmar Gromann, and Sebastian Rudolph. 2021. Neural machine translating from natural language to sparql. *Future Generation Computer Systems*, 117:510–519.

Author Index

Association for Computational Linguistics
209 N. Eighth Street
Stroudsburg, Pennsylvania 18360

ISBN 978-1-7138-6737-1

CURRAN ASSOCIATES INC. proceedings.com